The Texas Dogman Triangle

D1522585

Aaron Deese

The Texas Dogman Triangle

This edition published by Small Town Monsters Publishing, LLC in 2023

Author: Aaron Deese

Cover Art: Jonathan Dodd

Table of Contents

Dedication

For our son, Ezra Blaine.

Everything will always be for you.

Acknowledgements

This book would be naught but a fever dream, or perhaps, naught but nothing were I without the unending love and support of my wife, partner, best friend and mother-of-my-child, Sara.

It would be a criminal offense not to thank the numerous researchers, writers, investigators, podcasters, filmmakers, friends, family, and generally exceptional human individuals who contributed both directly and indirectly to the writing of this manuscript.

Ricky Deese, Lori Deese, Anicka Deese, Alysa Deese, Adana Mendoza, Camilla Mendoza, Marco Mendoza, Keith Straley, Linda Godfrey, Jeremiah Byron, Kenzie Gleason, Jessi Doyle, Joe Doyle, Sarah Cooper and the American Snallygaster Museum, Rod Nichols, Jack Kirby, Jonathan Dodd, Ashley Hilt, Pat O'Sullivan, Mike Garcia, Jon Gonzales, Lyle Blackburn, Michael Mayes, Jordan Heath, Michaela Ford, Danner Seyfur-Sprauge, Greg Morrill, Joedy Cook, Nick Valenzuela, Victor Rangel, Nick Redfern, Pam Hartmann, Richard Hartmann, Neil Tyrrell, Scott Baldwin, Christian Moore, Richard Krenz, Ken Gerhard, Shannon Legro, Courteney Swihart RVT, Trent Fulton, Alex Kipple, Leandro Castro III, Synthia Garcia, John, Raquel Paredes, Sara's and my six domestic cats, my friends and colleagues in the property management field who have listened to me incessantly prattle about werewolves for the last two years, attendees of various social gatherings wherein I hijacked the conversation by doing the exact same thing, Heather Moser (the best and most patient editor any person could ever ask for), BJ and Metra of Unrefined, Heather Corday, The Mothboys Podcast, Thomas of Highkey Obsessed Podcast, This Paranormal Life, Joss and Monique Rose of Fright Life Paranormal, Caleb Jones, Seth Breedlove and the rest of the Small Town Monsters team, Zac Palmisano, Eli

Watson, Homer Croy, Jim Butcher, Frank Herbert, Joe Abercrombie, John Keel.

Grandma Irene, who always believed that her weird grandson could write a book and reminded me every day that writing runs in the family. Rest well Grandma.

Foreword

When I was in high school, I had a girlfriend whose parents owned a lake house in East Texas. During our trips there we would often visit old cemeteries along the wooded backroads looking for ghosts or whatever strange and spooky thrills we could find. One night we came upon a particularly lonesome graveyard we had not seen before. It was well after dark and we had no flashlight, but the moon was full and bright enough to provide sufficient light for a quick exploration.

I parked my truck, and we entered through a rickety gate that seemed as old and tired as the smattering of weathered tombstones beyond it. I'm typically fearless in wooded settings, even in the dark, but I could tell my girlfriend wasn't as comfortable. She remained close to the gate while I walked to the back corner of the small, fenced-in spread trying to find the oldest grave markers. I began scanning a row of antiquated tombstones looking at the dates when a noise caught my attention. It came from a patch of thick pine trees just beyond the fence. Armadillos are often rooting around the Texas woods at night and can be quite noisy, however this was different. More reserved, stealthy perhaps. I remember peering into the deep shadows between the trunks and the undergrowth trying to see what was there. I felt certain it was some kind of animal when I heard it move yet again. There was a footstep or two, then silence, as if it were apprehensive of my presence or worse, just watching me from the darkness. It was then I heard a sound that still haunts me today. It was a cross between a grunt and a growl, loud, deep, and throaty. This thing was no armadillo, nor anything else I could grasp in that moment. The sound wasn't the grunt of a deer, the snort of a wild hog (as I have come to know very well), or the growl of a cat. It was more dog-like, perhaps wolfish, giving me the flash impression of some huge canid. I remember one word distinctly popped into my mind… *hellhound*.

The thought was enough to send me running for the cemetery gate, hollering at my girlfriend to get into the truck. I don't recall if she had heard the noise as well, but my panic was enough to trigger her into action. I cranked the truck engine, and we promptly left the area with a mixed feeling of fear and excitement. I've experienced some unsettling incidents in the woods over the years, but this was the only time I ever turned and ran. I never saw the animal that made the noise so I could only imagine what it could have been, if not a very large dog. Romantic notions of a werewolf came to mind, but surely that would have been impossible. I was in Texas, not Transylvania. There are no such lycanthropes lurking anywhere near the Lone Star State…or are there?

In the years that followed I became more interested in the study of cryptids (creatures said to exist although unproven) where I learned that sightings of such wolf-like creatures had taken place in modern times *and* in Texas. There were folkloric legends such as the Converse Werewolf dating back to the late 1800s, but these were far more recent encounters reported by people who could be verified and interviewed. Many times, these witnesses were not only shocked by the actual encounter, but surprised to learn that a creature resembling a werewolf could even be out there stalking the forests of Texas and beyond. Something us cryptid researchers refer to as a "Dogman" or "Dogmen."

In the last decade I've seen a drastic increase in Dogman reports, suggesting that either these alleged creatures are becoming bolder, breeding at an alarming rate, or people are becoming more comfortable sharing such stories. And that is perhaps the case. The time period of these encounters could be as recent as yesterday or something that happened decades ago. Telling someone you saw a "werewolf" is not always an easy thing given the potential for ridicule, so in some cases the witnesses had kept the story to themselves for many years. As each incident comes to light, it adds to the extensive file of anecdotal stories that suggest something akin to a werewolf may exist outside our current framework of understanding. I've interviewed first-hand witnesses myself and can assure you that even though it may sound impossible, there's enough tantalizing evidence to make this pursuit worthwhile.

As a native Texan, cryptid researcher, and lifelong fan of werewolf/wolfman movies (I even have a tattoo of Lon Chaney, Jr. as The Wolfman on my arm!), I was excited to learn that one of my colleagues was putting together a book about the Dogman phenomenon in Texas. And even better, I was asked to write the Foreword. It's a book I might have written myself, but one that I don't have to because we are in the capable hands of Aaron Deese. Deese and I met through our work with Small Town Monsters, where I was immediately impressed by his enthusiasm. And now reading this book, I'm impressed by his research and dedication to the subject of cryptozoology and Dogman in particular where he brings the Texas phenomenon into a sharp, triangular focus so that we can all learn something here. And perhaps find ourselves questioning what lurks in the Southern backwoods.

The subject of unexplained creatures is infinitely fascinating and can be equally terrifying when it comes to monstrosities such as living werewolves. So, sit back, grab a drink and a silver bullet if you like, and let's join Aaron for a hair-raising romp across the Texas woodlands and creeks in search of the truth behind Dogmen. Just make sure you're ready to run if you happen to hear a deep, throaty growl coming from the shadows during a full moon. It just might save your life!

Lyle Blackburn

March 2023

Introduction

While I have yet to obtain a specimen of the animal, I have seen its traces in all directions. - The Book of Werewolves by Sabine Baring Gould (1865)

Werewolf. Wolfman. Cynocephalus. Lycanthrope. Rougarou. Loup-garou. Skinwalker.

Dogman.

For untold centuries wolves posed an existential threat to human populations. A primordial boogeyman in many respects, the savage forebears of man's best friend have generally been anything but friendly. It takes little imagination to envision humans huddling around dying fires or in complete darkness, brandishing crudely formed weapons at the sound of bestial howls. The world was far more formidable without the conveniences of modern technology such as electricity, locking doors, fossil fuels, and firearms. Even in the current day, however, one can find examples of wolves setting upon human prey, and the outcome of these attacks is rarely positive.

Stories of wolves or wolf-like creatures inundate our literary and cultural histories. Across the globe, any geographical area wherein they are or were once native seems to have its share of pertinent mythologies. This is unsurprising, for human beings faced a much higher rate of mortality at the claws and teeth of savage predators than we do today. We no longer live alongside the wolves. By and large we no longer fear them, but our ancestors were not afforded the same luxury. The legacy of the monsters that haunted our precursors is preserved through countless legends, folktales, and myths.

The state of Texas is no exception. References to wolf populations can be found in the archives of many Texan newspapers: titles such as Wolf Mountain, Wolf

Creek, and Wolf Hill are popular names for natural locations, roads, and suburban neighborhoods. Although proper wolves have been extinct in Texas since the 1940s, they were once a dominant predatory figure of the Lone Star State. Hunted and culled with extreme prejudice, however, the southeastern red wolf and gray wolf no longer prowl the plains and forests of Texas with impunity. Even the great dire wolf, now totally extinct for all intents and purposes, once reigned over the cliffs and valleys of this daunting expanse.[1]

Due in part to the rich oral history of native peoples in this region, eventually blended with the folk tales of European settlers, the American southwest would become a hub for talk of another canine creature; a character which many consider naught but the fiction of Hollywood screenwriters or the imaginary villain of childhood nightmares. A horror which, in the modern-day, is synonymous with Dracula, Frankenstein's Monster, and Creature from the Black Lagoon. We refer, of course, to the werewolf.

Werewolf legends are nothing new and predate the birth of Lon Chaney, Jr. by centuries - even millennia. Since we discovered the means to turn pigment to image, mankind has recorded bipedal canines with such regularity that it becomes impossible not to ask why. There are countless depictions of such a creature. Anubis of ancient Egypt, who escorted deceased kings into the afterlife and presided as his father, Osiris, passed judgment on them. The Arcadian king Lykaon of Greek mythology, who was transformed into a wolf by Zeus as punishment for committing an act of cannibalism. The benevolent Wulver

---

[1] While some recent encounters may herald the eventual return of wild wolves to the state, they are yet to be considered properly native in the 21st century. As of 2022, however, no wild wolf populations are known to exist within the 268,000+ square miles between Mexico, Louisiana, Arkansas, Oklahoma, and New Mexico. Sort of.

of ancient Scotland, who would guide lost travelers back home and leave fish on the windowsills of the hungry. The savage werewolf - a warlock or witch in many respects - of the European Middle Ages, feared and reviled: the stuff of nightmares. Saint Christopher of the Catholic faith, portrayed in classical depictions as a dog headed holy-man-warrior. In fact, Saint Christopher is not the only cynocephalic creature painted by ecclesiastical artists. Other religious stories cast them in the roles of both hero and villain.

On the North American continent, we meet the Rougarou of the deep south, a creature descended from the folklore of the French which haunts the swamps and bayous of Louisiana. Then there is the Skinwalker of First Nations tribes, a dark creature whose name alone carries such weight that to speak it aloud is considered taboo. As a result, those not affiliated with tribes in question have only limited access to their oral traditions. Eventually, pop culture is inundated with incarnations of modern mythology in the form of films, video games, comic books, television shows, narrative podcasts, fantasy roleplaying games, young adult urban fantasy romance novels, and much more besides. Bipedal canines can be found throughout the world and throughout time, with little restriction given by place or period. They are portrayed as both malicious and well-meaning, dangerous, and protective, as savage beasts and intelligent sentients. The question of *"what is a werewolf?"* depends entirely upon who you ask and when you ask them.

Modern-day accounts given by credible witnesses would seem to place similar creatures in a variety of haunts, including the United States. Wisconsin, Michigan, and Oklahoma are three locations often discussed.

Naturally, they have also made a home in Texas. Many older stories in the vein of werewolves are scattered across the state, dating back a century or more. Incidents shared by living eyewitnesses add to the idea of bipedal canines in the American southwest, punctuated by bizarre newspaper articles from the mid-century. As recently as 2022, there are stories of them being seen in broad daylight, shot at, and captured on camera. Today these creatures are referred to by another name which has quickly gained traction and acceptance in the cryptozoology and paranormal communities: Dogman.

Dogman is discussed by researchers, enthusiasts, and experiencers as an actuality. This is a stark departure from the mythology of old and the deluge of contemporary incarnations which we can trace back to the 1941 film *The Wolfman*. Many of these individuals within the cryptozoology community have evidence to back up the growing belief that these things, these wolves that walk on two feet, might actually exist.

The Dogman is something of a cryptozoological anomaly. While the study of cryptids or unknown animals has traditionally been dominated by sasquatch research and a few other well-known creatures—the Beast of Busco, the hodag, the jackalope, and, of course, the ever-popular Mothman, for example—the Dogman has risen to prominence in more recent years. Advances in technology have unlocked a new world of possibilities for field research, and ongoing sightings have begun to make the case for the presence of a dog-like creature lurking somewhere in the shadows of North America. Because of this, researchers are seeing encounters attributed to Bigfoot in a new light, shifting the perspective of what people may be seeing. It might also be argued that there is a romanticism to the idea of "real werewolves" when the iconography is so heavily ingrained in modern pop culture. Such saturation has doubtlessly contributed to the Dogman's burgeoning popularity. Fictional depictions notwithstanding, there is a growing section of paranormal enthusiasts - and in truth, has been for quite a while - that continue to study the Dogman phenomena with sincere scientific interest. I have been fortunate enough to make the acquaintance of several of these researchers, and through my talks with them have gained a new appreciation for the breadth of the entity that is Dogman in the great state of Texas.

Jon Gonzales of *True Horror Stories of Texas*, a long-running and ever-expanding website devoted to encounters with the inexplicable in the state, notes, "I have seen more werewolf/Dogman style stories in the last couple years than when we first started."

Gonzales, who is a lifelong paranormal enthusiast and present-day theater teacher, started the website in 2016. Submitted reports from witnesses around the state have remained steady since the page's inception, describing everything from ghosts to UFOs to doppelgängers and much, much more. The website has a wealth of werewolf and/or Dogman encounters, most of which are not documented anywhere else (until their inclusion in this book). Perusing the comments left on these articles by readers yields even further anecdotes of similar sightings, and the website provided hours of research material during the draft of this volume.

Gonzales grew up near the border in the Rio Grande Valley, his upbringing steeped in the rich Mexican American culture of that region. Folklore played a significant role in the framing of his worldview, and he credits his mother as being the one who initially sparked his interest in the paranormal.

Another veteran of the unsolved is Joedy Cook, director of the North American Dogman Project. His organization gathers evidence of Dogman encounters from across the continent, and their website may contain the most comprehensive collection of publicly available data. Newspaper articles, photographs, footprints and claw marks, audio recordings, videos, eyewitness accounts -

virtually any type of evidence one can think of - is found in the archives of the NADP website.

On the topic of Dogman sightings in Texas, Joedy had this to say:

"Texas is a big area and there's a lot of reports. Texas was definitely one of the first states where you're getting multiple sightings. I'm talking about Wisconsin and Michigan and Ohio, you're getting stuff coming out of Texas. Dogman stuff was there, and no one was really paying too much attention to it, unless they ran across something. But these are the states where you're getting a whole lot of the information from."[2]

Texas is certainly a hub of strange activity, which we will examine more closely as we go. While home to cities that are contemporary in most respects, Texas is still proudly draped in the legacy of the Wild West. Rumors of buried treasure are abundant, and the state is peppered with ghost towns.[3] Texas has a legacy of strangeness. These anomalies can be traced as far back as the Mesoamerican tribes who lived here in centuries past and whose descendants remain to this day.

While examining Dogman encounters in this area, certain patterns emerged regarding behavior and appearance. Features such as glowing eyes, pointed ears, bipedal locomotion, and human-like screams. When compared with local folktales these patterns remain consistent. Perhaps even more interesting, many of these encounters coincide geographically not only with similar contemporary reports, but also with the rumors and campfire tales of werewolves told in times gone by. In this volume, we will examine as many of these encounters and

---

[2] It should be noted that quotes, eyewitness reports, newspaper articles, etc. will be reprinted here with very little editing so as not to take away from the original source or conversational style.

[3] Texas boasts over 500 ghost towns within its boundaries - the most of any state in the country!

stories as can be prudently done while we attempt to draw a line around the areas most inundated with them. Or really, three lines, defining what I have affectionately come to refer to as the Texas Dogman Triangle.

In attempting to numerate paranormal encounters of any sort in any place, one might find it helpful to place them on a map and create a visual representation. It was just such a map, featured on the North American Dogman Project website under the sub menu *Encounters*, which sparked my interest in arranging Texan Dogman sightings geographically. More specifically, it was the geographic overlap of two eyewitness encounters submitted to the NADP website, with a third previously unreported sighting. I was fortunate enough to receive this third encounter firsthand from the experiencer.[4]

Zooming out, one may observe a pattern of "dogged" concentration in the central part of the state. As such, we can place cases relevant to this inquiry into two categories - those inside the triangle, and those outside of it. Additionally, I have found it helpful to classify these encounters into three categories: folkloric, anecdotal, and evidentiary.[5]

---

[4] These cases are detailed later in this volume, in a chapter titled *The Wolf Mountain Cluster.*

[5] Admittedly, most of the incidents we examine fall into the category of anecdotal. Behind that, we see numerous folkloric accounts, Finally, we have a smaller sampling of evidentiary encounters which are defined by photographic evidence, footprints, and other tangible "proofs" of strange, physical activity. Some evidentiary encounters are detailed in newspaper articles, but it is difficult to argue that these are not also anecdotal in nature.

Inside the Triangle

Folkloric
1) Cleo - The Beast of Bear Creek
2) Converse - The Converse Wolfman

Anecdotal
1) Johnson City (Pedernales Falls State Park)
2) Lampasas
3) Fredericksburg
4) Meridian
5) Freestone
6) Collin
7) Sam Houston National Forest (multiple)
8) Vidor
9) Lockhart - The Beast of Bear Creek
10) Sanger
11) Paradise
12) Orange
13) Conroe
14) Medina

Evidentiary
1) Near Dallas/Fort Worth

Outside the Triangle

Folkloric
1) Greggton

Anecdotal
1) Bluetown
2) McAllen
3) Roscoe

Evidentiary
1) San Benito
2) Amarillo

It becomes easy to see why the borders of the triangle are so defined. Inside this hypothetical territory are seventeen individual encounters - or, more academically, *potential* encounters - with upright canines. Taken one at a time, any of these tales may be written off to a variety of mundane explanations, such as hallucination, intoxication, misidentification, hyperbole, hoax, or copycat. There are reasons for and reasons against all of these being the cause of any cryptid encounter, and there are just as many counterarguments to write-off the write-offs. It is an endless cycle of *what if*. The purpose of this volume is not to convince one that werewolves exist - of that I am already certain and will explain why at a later time - but rather, it is to indicate that *something* is happening in a specific area with regard to a specific phenomenon, and to encourage the observer to ask their own questions.

I believe the state of Texas is home to some kind of canine species which defies currently known animal biology. I am reasonably confident that this creature can and at times does move on two legs, for purposes yet to be fully identified. Rather than try to convince the reader to agree with me, I will present the evidence to you as I have encountered it; and, once again, I encourage you to draw your own conclusions. While this theory may not account for every story detailed in this book, it does cover a satisfactory majority.

If nothing else, we will dive into some of the more obscure folklore of the Texas Hill Country. Some of it is very old and some is as recent as the year 2022. We will also toe the line into other avenues of strangeness in the Lone Star State with the hope of giving the reader a more comprehensive picture of what a truly Fortean place the

American Southwest is. The stories in this book are presented not in chronological order but rather are arranged as they relate to one another by means of location and common themes.

It is probably safe to assume that the majority of people in the world do not believe in werewolves. No straw polls were conducted during the creation of this manuscript, but the numerous eyebrows raised in incredulous expression have made it clear that disbelief and doubt are often the case. To be transparent, when I first ran across this concept as a category of cryptozoological inquiry, my immediate response was *yeah, right*.[6] My opinion of werewolves was the same as that of many others: the idea was laughable and pure fiction at that.

But time passed, evidence stacked on evidence, and I became engrossed in the writings of authors Linda S. Godfrey and Nick Redfern. Through my former capacity as a writer for Paranormality Magazine I became acquainted with numerous figures in the paranormal, cryptozoological, and unsolved communities. The conversations resulting from these acquaintances challenged my perspective. I stumbled upon web articles on several sites detailing run-ins with what the witnesses believed were upright walking canines, and I noticed several patterns in these articles which were consistent from source to source. Before too long, I had noted enough activity in Texas purported to be connected to wolfmen, or, at the very least, weird dogs to fill a book, and my friend Jeremiah recommended that I do just that.

This is that book.

---

[6] I had long been familiar with the Chupacabra, Sasquatch, the Loch Ness Monster, and some others, of course, but this canid category was new to me.

1

Texas: A Backdrop of Strangeness

The Lone Star State is a unique expanse of territory. It has the distinction of being home to a presidential assassination and six formerly independent nations. That's not to mention, it is also a deep well of paranormal, supernatural, and superstitious folklore. It is miles upon square miles of diverse environments, from the soaked terrain to desert. The sun shines bright over the arid plains and gives dense growth to the forest-flanked rivers of the Hill Country. The rain often floods the lowest reaches, while periodic wildfires ravage it during the dry seasons. Hurricanes batter the coast, and in 2021 Texas even played host to a devastating blizzard. It has become home to cowboys, oil magnates, madams, entrepreneurs, inventors, ranchers, revolutionaries, war heroes, scientists, presidents, writers and so on. Texas breeds some of the most interesting creatures, and while the adage *Everything is Bigger in Texas* may be a tired cliche, the state has more than one right to ownership of the phrase.

As mentioned, it also bears what many may consider to be an inordinate amount of the strange and inexplicable. Ghosts, aliens, cryptids, conspiracy, true crime, hidden treasure - all are magnificently represented. A great length of time and research may be devoted to any one of these topics, and the researcher need not venture too far outside the borders of Texas - indeed, need not venture out at all - to be overwhelmed. On the topic of ghosts: the haunted halls of Seguin, Austin, San Antonio, Dallas, Houston, and dozens more have filled a multitude of books. UFOs are numerous as well: the Lubbock Lights, the Aurora Crash, the San Antonio Cylinders, and the Baker

Mayfield sighting just to name a few. There are Sasquatch reports and sightings across the state: unsurprisingly thickest near Texarkana and Fouke, Arkansas (home of the famous Boggy Creek Monster), but also even across the highways of the ever-growing expanse of San Antonio.

To comprehensively address all prime examples in every category would take several volumes. To set the stage for this book, however, we will examine an area well within the borders of the Texas Dogman Triangle. This is one of many "hot spots" scattered throughout the state, and it is close to several of the strange encounters examined elsewhere in this book. It is a made-man reservoir surrounded by rolling valleys, thick vegetation, and a burgeoning civilian population: Lake Travis.

The Lake Travis Window

Between Lampasas and Johnson City is a stretch of the westernmost border of north Austin. Here sits Lake Travis, one of the largest bodies of water in the central Texas area. Lake Travis has its own history of the strange, unsolved, and, in some cases, tragic. Since 1941 the Mansfield Dam has held the Colorado River in check, giving form to Lake Travis and creating a space for lakeside properties, fishing, swimming, boating, paddle boarding, and other family-friendly activities.

Rumors have circulated for years of alligators dwelling in the murky depths of the reservoir. Generally, their origin is attributed to a lakeside Austin resident who adopted (perhaps through less than legitimate means) a breeding pair of the reptiles and then released them into the waters of Lake Travis when they became too difficult to care for. This trope is a common story in some places (Florida, specifically) but it somehow seems stranger against the backdrop of the American southwest. Like most urban legends, the stories included exaggerated accounts of the gigantic killer reptiles devouring dogs and, in some cases, unlucky humans. While no hard evidence could be found to corroborate the tales, at least one alligator was to be found deceased on the shores of Lake Travis in 2011. This serves to confirm, at least to a minor extent, the rumors - there were, in fact, unaccounted for alligators living in Lake Travis. Even if the one known to have perished was the only example - which would seem unlikely - their presence as a non-native species to the environment has now been proven. This falls in line with the very definition of cryptozoology - the investigation and discovery of unknown animals. In some cases, such study includes animals unknown to the environments in which they are found. For example, tales of "Phantom Big Cats" have abounded in the UK and US for years, despite official government agencies denouncing such claims. Alligators in Texas, it now seems, are squarely in the same realm.

Over the last few decades, numerous people have gone missing - truly missing, their bodies never recovered - on Lake Travis. With occurrences as recent as 2005, those missing range from kayakers to swimmers to weekend boaters. Caution must be taken not to appropriate human tragedy with a ghoulish interest in the paranormal, and the families of many of those missing are still alive today. Out of respect for those missing and their loved ones, this topic will not be examined further here. This item is mentioned because these cases do have things in common with other accounts of strange disappearances, including the oft discussed Missing 411 discussion popularized by investigator and author David Paulides, which contributes to the total weight of weirdness in this lush aquatic getaway.

Lake Travis in 2021. Photo by the author.

In 2020, then Cleveland Browns Quarterback Baker Mayfield and his wife Emily Wilkinson witnessed what Mayfield described as a large, bright object descending from the sky over Lake Travis. Mayfield was quoted in numerous publications about the incident, even going on to say that he believes in the existence of beings such as Sasquatch. This modern-day account not only featured multiple witnesses who readily came forward with the story (Emily also remarked upon the sighting on her Twitter account), but also it marks a rare example of a person already in the public spotlight admitting to an encounter with the paranormal. Celebrity does not necessarily denote credibility, but it does demonstrate the willingness of Mr. Mayfield to subject himself to public ridicule. Why bother doing so for a fabricated story?

The writer was fortunate enough to witness an illuminated object traveling at high speeds in the Lake Travis area as recently as 2022. While I made a pre-midnight run to Taco Bell, a bluish-white light moved away from Lake Travis, well above the treetops or any nearby structures, before coming to an abrupt halt and descending rapidly over a heavily wooded area. The first and still most likely explanation for this sighting is that of a drone.

Problems with this explanation are few but significant. First, use of drones within the city of Austin without special permission is illegal. While this will not stop many from flying their personal aircraft regardless of the rule of law, it does diminish the likelihood of any given (or at least some) drone operators being the source of the moving light. It should be noted that, as of 2022, Austin police will no longer issue citations for use of drones within city limits, at least during the finalization of FAA regulations.

In addition, the light moved with striking speed and precision. To operate an unmanned aerial vehicle of any size at such a height and with complete disregard for wind resistance would be challenging at best. While there are certainly in existence drone operators who possess the ability, there are limitations to the most modern of drone technology. Finally, the height at which the light traveled parallel to the earth must also be considered. An emergency services helicopter may travel at an average height of 1000 feet. According to an FAA fact sheet found at nifc.gov, the maximum allowable height of an unmanned aerial vehicle is 400 feet "and higher if your drone remains within 400 feet of a structure." This fact sheet seems to pertain specifically to military equipment but does provide a point of reference for average drone elevation. The craft witnessed by the author was likely traveling above 400 feet while proceeding in a straight line. Drone or not, the sight was striking, and these two examples are not the only UFO/UAP sightings which Lake Travis can boast.

Another odd encounter took place allegedly in 2007. A photograph was shared on Reddit depicting a man with his back to the camera, facing a body of water at night.

On the far left is a boat docked by the shore, and on the right… something else.

The original photo has been shared dozens of times online but is believed to originate on Reddit.

The observer can clearly see a bipedal figure lit by the flash of the camera in use. Eyeshine twinkles bright on the figure's face. A shaggy length of fur or maybe the excess material of a mask or shawl frame the creature's eyes. Or is it a mane? A bushy matting of hair? Two arms are visible, as are two legs, and portions of the torso are partially covered.

I recently recirculated this photo on social media channels and received a variety of interesting hypotheses regarding what may be in the photo. No one knows for sure, but we are left to speculate: Is this a feral human? Scantily clothed, exceptionally tall vagrant? Costumed actor? Alien? Ghost? Dogman? Sasquatch? Djinn? Elemental? Fae? Demon? A Pukwudgie with gigantism?

No explanation is presently off the table. Since its initial appearance in 2007 the photograph has been often discussed and repeatedly debunked, but no popular explanation is generally accepted. Attempts to contact the original owner of the photograph - allegedly a "biology professor" - have thus far proven unfruitful. Explanations from various Reddit threads and comment chains on blogs reporting on the sighting seem to agree that the figure must be "11-14 feet tall" based upon its proximity and height relative to the human subject in the foreground. Additional data would seem, at present, to be unavailable.

Admittedly, Lake Travis has not - at least at writing - played host to any known Dogman encounters other than the possible one shown above. But this strange, potential "window area" is located near the center of the Texas Dogman Triangle, encompassing the hills and forests of far west Austin, and to ignore its presence would be a lazy course at best. Future study and observation of the Lake Travis area is not only advisable but begins to seem necessary when these assorted oddities are considered.

This is saying nothing of the saturation of ghosts in San Antonio, the Black-Eyed Kids and phantom specters of Abilene, the various cryptid sightings in Dallas/Fort Worth, nor the paranormal hotbed of Floresville (of which I have only recently become aware). Galveston is haunted by the ghosts of infamous pirates, and Donna is known as the "Ghost Capital" of the state. Port Arthur was founded by a man who believed that he regularly communicated with fae-like entities he referred to as "Brownies." There is the inexplicable red glow of the Marfa Lights, the many Bigfoot sightings around Jefferson, the Martian's grave in Aurora, the Batman of Houston, tales of La Lechuza near the border, and many, many more.

We will touch on some of these areas and their various odd happenings in exploration of the topic at hand, but it is my hope that by profiling one location in detail, the reader may gain some understanding of just how strange the state of Texas is.

2

Strange Canines

You talk to old timers in Texas, and they'll tell you they've seen strange creatures that fit the description that's now assigned to 'Chupacabra' (Texas Terror Dog) for a long time. - Kristina Downs, The Texas Folklore Society

Our primary interest is in the upright variety of wolf-beast, but there are other examples of regional canines which defy expectation. Both past and present display examples which run contrary to the generally accepted database of fauna, and whose very existence is - or once was - considered gossip and myth. They are steeped in both science and folklore tracing roots back further than we can determine. In some of these cases, scientists have analyzed samples of their DNA.

Terrible Dogs in Texas

The Texas Terror Dog, also called the Texas Chupacabra, first gained widespread infamy in 2007. In the early days of "viral" content, a series of videos, along with features on the evening news, claimed that a gruesome dog-like creature was making appearances in southwest Texas. This beast was even spotted feeding on the blood of livestock - specifically chickens. Before cable networks could produce several documentary TV features on the phenomenon - which they later did - the creature had come to be known as the "Texas Chupacabra." A few savvy entrepreneurs made a small fortune on T-shirts and other merchandise when the buzz around the animal was at its height, and the money-making marquee value of the name may have played a role in its application to the beast in question.

Efforts have been made in the interim to distinguish the creature from the original Chupacabra of Puerto Rico - an altogether separate monstrosity, with little to no resemblance to any canine. After all, the creatures seen in the American Southwest are generally described as canines with little or no body hair and a somewhat ghastly, likely diseased appearance. The Chupacabra of Puerto Rico is described as looking something like a cross between a monkey and lizard, is sometimes portrayed as having wings, and is also often compared to the large-headed bulging-eyed alien grays which are now so familiar to us.

The result of this discontent with the moniker was the name *Texas Terror Dog*, which is growing in popularity throughout facets of the paranormal community. The name was put forth by Joss and Monique Rose of the podcast *Fright Life Paranormal* as a part of a campaign sponsored by *Paranormality Magazine*. Votes were tallied after a six-week series of brackets, and from a wide pool of proposed titles, *Texas Terror Dog* emerged victorious. Support for the campaign was bolstered by the *Cryptozoology Club* group on the social networking app *Clubhouse* (run by Jeremiah Byron of *The Bigfoot Society Podcast*), and the idea of renaming the creature was initially proposed by cryptozoologist and paranormal investigator Kenzie Gleason. Since then, support for the new name has been expressed by Seth Breedlove, Lyle Blackburn, David Weatherly, Aleks Petakov, Sarah Cooper, Heather Moser, and many, many more.

How long this creature has been a part of the ecosystem of Texas is anyone's guess, but modern specimens subjected to DNA testing have yielded results indicating a mixture of domestic dog, coyote, and Mexican wolf DNA. Some of the first modern sightings of this creature are accounted for in Elmendorf, just south of San Antonio and less than 20 miles from the southernmost border of the Texas Dogman Triangle. Much consideration was given to including Texas Terror Dog activity as a part of the Dogman Triangle, but to do so would open a proverbial can of worms and would certainly invite controversy. In truth, the creature does not fit the profile of atypical Dogman sightings. However, like the werewolf archetype, the Texas Terror Dog has likely been with us since much earlier than 2007.

Dr. Kristina Downs is the Executive Director of the Texas Folklore Society. She is also an assistant professor of English at Tarleton University and was kind enough to speak with me about strange happenings and extraordinary beings in our shared state of residence.

"You talk to old timers in Texas, and they'll tell you they've seen strange creatures that fit the description that's now assigned to 'Chupacabra' (Texas Terror Dog) for a long time. They just didn't have a name for it. Now any time anyone sees anything that has four legs and is kind of weird looking, it gets called 'Chupacabra.'"

We discussed the Texas Terror Dog (aka Texas Chupacabra) at length. Regarding the recent introduction of Texas Terror Dog as an alternate and perhaps improved title for the creature, Kristina had this to say:

"If you look at - and I'm by no means an expert on Chupacabra lore - but it obviously gets referred to as the Mexican Goat Sucker even though it comes out of Puerto Rico - but the early descriptions aren't really that dog-like. I think putting 'dog' in the name maybe helps fit the description of what we are seeing come out of this area."

Kristina has an impressive pool of knowledge regarding the history and folklore of Texas, including many of its stranger aspects. She and I seemed to agree that there is a vast wealth of odd stories scattered across the state, and she made mention of the overwhelming number of "Buried

Treasure" legends that Texas boasts. While this may not be considered "paranormal," it certainly adds to the intrigue of the backdrop. Naturally our conversation turned towards Sasquatch at a point, as discussions pertaining to cryptozoology and folklore often do.

"I'm a skeptical believer. I believe in the possibility of all these things but then I have to stop and go *well... I don't know.*"

Kristina provided a fascinating example of otherworldly dog-like creatures of which I had previously not heard. Like the Texas Terror Dog, these supernatural hounds were also given to quadrupedal locomotion.

Hellhounds and Black Dogs

"This particular story seems to fall in more of a religious direction," Kristina said.

"The story is that a man was in the woods and was chased by what he describes as *Hellhounds,* and literally wandered into Hell. He slipped through some kind of portal, into Hell, and had this encounter of the hounds continuing to chase him through the different levels of Hell until he escaped and returned to Earth."

When asked where this encounter transpired, Kristina recalled the report coming from the area of "far east Texas, or maybe over the border in Arkansas."

Portals, evil hounds, and a journey through the layers of Hell. There are elements here from a variety of traditional texts and fables, and one cannot help but be reminded of Dante's *Inferno.* Oddly enough, this is not the only story of Hellhounds emerging from portals in the state.

Black Dogs or Hellhounds as a phenomenon should be considered their own category and have associated legends spanning the globe. Often a bad omen or sign of ill fortune, they are generally described as malevolent beings to be avoided whenever possible. We find them in force in the Lone Star State.

A story which very well may be a creepypasta, or internet urban legend, tells of a girl in El Paso, Texas whose family was slaughtered by evil black dogs which emerged from a portal on the family's land. The home had apparently once belonged to practitioners of dark magic who sacrificed animals to the Devil.

And still the Hounds of Hell march on.

In the 2010 book *Monsters of Texas*, which was co-authored by Nick Redfern and Ken Gerhard, there is a striking encounter with a suspected Hellhound near the city of Amarillo, located in the far North of Texas in the state's "panhandle." Amarillo is also a feature of the Dogman narrative in our exploration, but we will return there later.

This story was shared with Redfern by a witness identified as Ronda who was visiting Paladora State Park with her daughter and son-in-law when they saw something that sent all three on a retreat towards home.

The tale goes that as the three were enjoying a picnic on a gorgeous afternoon, taking in the scenery of the majestic retreat, one of them noticed they were being watched by a massive black dog. The story does not say which of the three first took notice of the huge canine which watched them from "200 to 300" yards, but, at some point, one of them did. The hound was "the size of a small horse" and had eyes that shone silver. The creature charged, ostensibly growing more fearsome in appearance as it drew closer.

The trio fled. No mention is made of whether they collected their picnic or left it for the dog, but the beast apparently stalked them all the way back to their vehicle. Their hellish encounter concludes with the creature moving close to a replica of a Native American teepee and then vanishing into thin air.

Consulting the internet would seem to yield no results for Paladora State Park, but there is a Palo Duro State Park just south of Amarillo which is home to the second longest canyon in the United States. It is consistent with the location described in Ronda's encounter, and Paladora is very likely a typo on the part of the publisher or copyeditor.

There is yet another Hellhound legend in the Lone Star State. This one is grounded in at least some verifiable and documented history. One might look to the Maison Rouge in Galveston, TX, one-time home of the infamous pirate Jean Lafitte.

Maison Rouge - or Red House - was once an extravagant combination mansion and fortress. There is perhaps no better description of the house than the one embossed on the plaque of the Texas State Historical Survey Committee which currently sits on the property:

Jean Lafitte
Notorious pirate settled here in 1817 with his buccaneers and ships under Mexican flag, continued his forays against Spanish shipping in the Gulf.

On this site, he built his home, Maison Rouge (Red House), which was part of his fort, and upper story was pierced for cannon. It was luxuriously furnished with booty from captured ships.

Leaving Galveston in 1821, upon demand of the United States, he burned his home, fort and whole village, then sailed to Yucatan.

In 1870, present structure was built over old cellars and foundations of Maison Rouge (1965)

The Maison Rouge in 2022

Today, it sits in a deceptively nondescript alleyway off Harborside Drive tucked between palm trees, undergrowth, and newer structures which may as well exist in another dimension. While only minutes from the Galveston beach, the small plot of land is truly an artifact of another time. Upon our visit, an easily scalable or crawl-underable chain link fence with a light coat of rust presented as the only obstacle towards physically entering the structure, but a personal distaste for trespassing and tetanus prevented this. Despite temptation.

What makes this location significant here is the rumored existence of a supernatural pack of malevolent black dogs: The Campeche Devil Dogs.

The story goes that Jean Lafitte commissioned a voodoo priestess to supernaturally endow a pack of bloodthirsty hounds - in some versions, an undefined hybrid of the "Spanish Black Wolf" - to pursue his enemies and guard Maison Rouge. In one telling of the legend, the pack had grown to be over 500 strong by the time Lafitte abandoned his fortress and fled to Yucatan. Supposedly, Lafitte left the dogs behind - one can imagine the logistics of sailing across the Mexican Gulf with 500 dogs - and their spirits are said to linger to this day. There are whispers of modern-day Galveston residents and visitors alike seeing large black silhouettes with glowing red eyes, smelling wet dog fur, and hearing growls and snarls when visiting Maison Rouge. Perhaps even stranger still, these phenomena are not limited to Lafitte's former residence, but are repeated in other places once frequented by Jean Lafitte such as his Blacksmith Shop - now a tavern built from the original stone walls - in New Orleans, LA.

These are not the only strange canines to haunt the island of Galveston. Animals with a mix of DNA from various canid species, including the Mexican red wolf have been reported in and around Galveston as far back as 2008. These hybrids have received ample media coverage, even being featured in such publications as the New York Times. Might there be some connection between these modern-day mutts and Lafitte's Devil Dogs? Additionally, is there some link between the presence of Mexican red wolf DNA in both the Texas Terror Dog and the "Galveston Wolves"? Perhaps not, but to ignore the possibility would be to forego a fascinating line of inquiry. Whatever the answers to either of these questions, it would seem undeniable that at some level, wolves are making a slow and triumphant return to the Lone Star State, even if only in the form of previously unknown wolfish amalgamations.

As a tangential aside, there is the Jean Lafitte National Historical Park in modern-day Louisiana named for the notorious pirate. The Barataria Nature Preserve is a part of the expanse and contains over 26,000 acres which were also once home to red wolves. Like their Texan cousins, they have since been extirpated. Louisiana is rife with its own werewolf lore, but a deep dive into this area is not possible herein. The beastly Rougarou, as the monster is known regionally in the Bayou State, is easily its own book and then some.

These strange canines neither prove nor disprove the idea of a bipedal wolf in Texas. However, in a relatively short space we have discussed five examples of mythological hounds and/or confirmed hybrid canines; The Texas Terror Dog, The Campeche Black Dogs, the Hellhounds of Eastern Texas, El Paso, and Amarillo, and, of course, the Galveston Wolves. A mixture of ghost stories, cryptid mythos, and modern folklore with examples of scientific data cross bred (pun intended) into some of the more exotic elements of the stories. The tangential relations between these tales and the idea of Dogman in Texas is impossible to ignore and should not be overlooked by any interested party.

3

The Sasquatch Connection

*Six-, seven-foot, eight-foot-tall hair-covered monsters...
the idea that believing there's even one out there is
hard enough to swallow for most people.* - Michael
Mayes

What if They're Just Primates?

Bigfoot has a long and complicated relationship
with the state of Texas. In discussions of Dogmen,
contrasts to sightings of Sasquatch are inevitable, arising in
almost every instance if one is discussed for long enough.
Many of the experts interviewed for this book have made
similar comparisons.

Ask any researcher who has spent time on the topic,
and they will happily tell you that Texas is a hot spot of
Sasquatch activity. Reports can be found all throughout the
state from a variety of sources, and to examine them in
detail would require more writing than this chapter will
allow. Suffice to say that sightings of strange bipeds,
anecdotes of wildmen/wildwomen and stories of ape-like
monsters abound. Prominent authors, researchers, and
filmmakers - many of whom contributed to the writing of
this book - have devoted considerable time, energy, and
resources into asking the Sasquatch question in the state of
Texas. There have even been several high-profile hoaxes,
one of which we will explore later.

Philanthropist Thomas Baker Slick, Jr. lived much
of his life in San Antonio. The inventor, author, and heir to
an oil fortune directed and financed cryptozoological
expeditions into Sumatra, Scotland, and Northern
California (perhaps better known to enthusiasts of the

unsolved niche as the Pacific Northwest). Slick also founded and bankrolled numerous scientific and speculative institutions. The Mind Science Foundation was created by Slick essentially to research the phenomena of psychic ability in humans. He also founded the Southwest Research Institute, which operates a primate testing facility (among many other ventures, such as testing of non-lethal weapons for military and law enforcement, as featured on the History Channel program *Modern Marvels*) as recently as 2022.

A metal Sasquatch cut out, serving as an homage to Slick's legacy, is displayed on the Institute's property. There will be more to say of the Southwest Research Institute later in this volume, and given the time, an entire book might be devoted to its examination.

The SWRI Sasquatch, courtesy of The Southwest Research Institute

San Antonio is also home to Tom Slick Park. The land was donated to the City of San Antonio out of Slick's master parcel known as Cable Ranch, current home to the SWRI. The park features art installations depicting the Loch Ness Monster as a metal statue in the middle of the pond, and Sasquatch footprints painted along one of the paved walkways. In addition, there are numerous roads in San Antonio labeled Cable Ranch Road, or byways adorned with similar signs sporting similar titles.

It is difficult (see: impossible) to summarize the adjacency of San Antonio to the paranormal with brevity. The reader is encouraged to examine this area at their convenience.

Jefferson, Texas proudly hails itself as the Bigfoot Capital of the state and has been the location of numerous sightings throughout the decades. Since 1991 Jefferson has annually hosted the Texas Bigfoot Conference. Speakers, vendors, and film screenings draw hundreds of visitors every year.

The Hairy Man of Round Rock, the Kelly Air Force Base sightings of the 70s, and many, many more contribute to the pile. There is even a town called Bigfoot with a population of less than 500 just south of San Antonio, though there is no known connection to cryptozoological phenomena. Rather, the town was named as an homage to Civil War veteran and notorious outdoorsman Bigfoot Wallace. Wallace also once made his home on the slopes now known as Mount Bonnel in West Austin, another location which is purportedly haunted. Any one of these instances makes for interesting reading, and the preceding examples are but a very, very small chip off an extremely large block. This is saying nothing of the more northern areas, closer to Dallas, Fort Worth, Houston, and the rural bounds at the edge of Louisiana and Oklahoma. In short, Texas is rife with Sasquatch. The unknowable wood ape is as much a part of the state as longhorns, creeks, tacos, and The San Antonio Spurs (a basketball team, in case one is not aware).

Rod Nichols is a San Antonio based paranormal investigator and cryptozoologist. A fan of such programs as *In Search Of* during childhood, Rod has always had a love for the unsolved. As a child his mother's friend was a close associate of Whitely Streiber, and he was introduced to the seminal volume *Communion* at a young age. He is also the creator of Bexar County Bigfoot. He has been investigating strange activity in Texas with a focus on San Antonio for more than four years, and in that time has come across a variety of interesting finds such as footprints measuring 14-16 inches in length, elaborate wood structures in isolated areas, and unidentifiable strange noises in the middle of the night. Rod has documented his discoveries through photograph and video, and his evidence is available to view online by anyone. I was fortunate enough to connect with him via social media. I asked Rod for his opinion on potential Dogman activity in the San Antonio area, and he relayed the following:

   "The tracks that I have seen and that I've witnessed and documented are all five-toed tracks, ranging from fourteen to sixteen inches long, and about six to seven inches wide at the toe box. To my knowledge the Dogman tracks are a little different. There's this whole debate on whether Sasquatch has a midtarsal break or not. Some people say they do, some people say they don't. The midtarsal break is found in primates... the Dogman tracks, from what I understand, have fewer toes... And there's evidence of claws that are around the toes to say well 'that's a Dogman, that's a dog track.' "

   A distinct anatomical feature would seem a good starting point for separating these two entities. But Rod does not dismiss the presence of two-legged dog-animals outright and makes a compelling case for the possibility.

   "It's possible. I live near one of the main creeks in North Central San Antonio, and if you know anything about that area it goes all the way up past (highway) loop

1604, outside the city and into a vast, thick, big, forested area. There's hills, there's a lot of creek. It feeds all the way smack dab into the city, so the whitetail come down through the creek for feeding and foraging. You've got a habitat that supports big game, and you've got a water source about a half mile away. That type of habitat is prime for Sasquatch."

The undeveloped tracts of San Antonio are indeed a wild environment. Nestled amidst the wards of a cosmopolitan metropolis which grows by the month - the city is home to almost 2.5 million residents as of 2022 - the rugged sections of the River City stretch for miles and feed into the prairie and hills beyond. Rod is not mistaken to categorize them as the prime environment of an unclassified apex animal.

"So, it makes sense," Rod says. "It makes sense that these creatures could go through these creeks like a highway that goes in and out of the city. It's a lot of creek, and it's connected to four other wilderness parks with more acreage, more whitetail deer. They've got a lot of things they can do. They can hunt, they can keep concealed. It's a thick greenbelt."

Debate is ongoing in the cryptozoological community as to the nature of Sasquatch's diet, but Rod is more than able to back up his supposition that the animal is predatory in nature.

"The reason I say they hunt is that I once found a deer carcass - a doe - that had been ripped apart. And it was decomposing - things had eaten off of it. The head was pulled off of the neck, and the head itself was pulled apart at the jaws. One half was on the other side, one half over here. And in the middle of the back, the spine was broken. So, I brought a wildlife biologist with me who took an interest in what I was doing. He took the carcass and tried to piece it together...and in the middle of the back it's *really* bowed back... and he said, 'something with force broke it's back right in half. I couldn't tell you what it is.'

"We don't have bears here. We don't have big cats. So, what is it? A person? And he said, 'that would be one strong person.'"

Rod supports his research with a comprehensive knowledge of the area's geological complexities.

"To add more to this, that area is an Edwards Aquifer recharge zone. It stretches all the way up to Austin. What we know is that we get our water from it, and they know a lot about that underground cavern. But do we truly know every piece of it? Do we truly know how deep it is? I don't think we do - I really don't think we do. I think we have a good idea, but I don't think we know exactly how deep and how vast it is."

Rod's theory is that the Sasquatch population in this area use the Edwards Aquifer caverns as a sort of underground main street. Using the concealment of the caverns, the access to food sources and a limitless supply of fresh water, they might remain undetected while literally walking under the feet of San Antonio's human population. The aquifer is a vast underground reservoir that runs through Texas and on into Oklahoma and Arkansas. Locally, the Natural Bridge Caverns, a privately owned state historical site, allows visitors a first-hand glimpse of a tiny portion of this sprawling underground world.

Could there be yet-unclassified ape-like creatures living in and beneath the San Antonio area, which utilize the unknowable depths of the Edwards Aquifer as a water source and transit route? Could an entity we might describe as Dogman - a bipedal canine, with the same biological needs as any corporeal life form - utilize this same natural highway?

"Could there be Dogmen running around here? I would not rule it out, at all. I would not be surprised if somebody had a Dogman encounter in the Bexar County area or even around Austin or Travis County."

When Rod and I conducted our first interview in June of 2022, we could not have guessed that he was speaking predictively. In December of 2022, Rod discovered a large canine-like print within the same system of creeks where he has documented other strange activity.

Unidentified canine print next to men's US size 10 shoe

This would do more than force me to raise an eyebrow. The print is shown here compared to an American size 10 men's shoe and is easily comparable in width. The creature which made it would also have to be of significant weight. It cannot be precluded that some other human visitor to the forest made the print intentionally or even by accident, but its presence in this area cannot be overlooked.

On Canines and Primates

A theory one frequently hears while investigating this topic is that sightings of Dogmen or werewolves are likely witnesses misidentifying Sasquatch with an untrained eye. This aspect of the Sasquatch connection cannot be overlooked, and I asked several people who I believe to be powerful forces in the field of the esoteric for their take on this idea.

Michael Mayes is an author and cryptozoologist. He is the creator of the *Texas Cryptid Hunter* blog, which has been active since 2008 and continues to be updated through present day. His most recent book, *Valley of The Apes: The Hunt for Sasquatch in Area X* is an in-depth investigation of the Bigfoot phenomena and is the product of years of research. He is also the chairman of the board of directors for the North American Wood Ape Conservancy, a Bigfoot research group, and he is actively involved in the organization's ongoing work. Growing up in the Texas Hill Country, Michael heard many horrifying stories around the campfire as a boy scout, and among those told to him were tales of terrifying monsters, savage beasts, and unknown preternatural nightmares. As an adult, Michael has taken a closer look at some of these folktales, viewing them through the lens of cryptozoology coupled with his own experiences. His website is a treasure trove, and his books are valuable resources. He has even published a children's book based on the famous Patterson Gimlin Sasquatch film and has worked as an educator for more than thirty years.

"Six-, seven-foot, eight-foot-tall hair-covered monsters… the idea that believing there's even one out there is hard enough to swallow for most people, much less that there could be more than one. A lot of the theories that I subscribe to are that we're probably seeing the same thing." Michael says.

But he adds,

"Now, I don't know - some people swear that they've seen the snout, so I don't know. There are a couple of good stories that would kind of fall in this category."

I also asked Lyle Blackburn, long-time figure of the cryptozoological field (as well as noted musician and hot sauce connoisseur) for his take on this idea.

"I think that has to do with people's existing beliefs about these creatures, and then how they want to try to explain the two varieties. If it's a Bigfoot researcher I find that often they'll say 'well, these are people who are misidentifying Bigfoot, there's no such thing as Dogman, it's just a big hairy Sasquatch.'"

Lyle continues,

"People who are whole hog into Dogman - whole dog into Dogman (*laughs*) - they just kind of disregard the Sasquatch connection and are more about this being a cryptid wolf that can walk upright, or more drastic, like some sort of interdimensional being and all that stuff. And the thing is, there's no doubt in my mind that Dogman has become sort of a trend, because having done this for so long you hardly heard about any Dogman sightings. It was the Beast of Bray Road and a few other random ones. Ten or twenty years ago, no one talked about it. Then there started to be more reports of Dogmen in the last five years, and all of a sudden it was like everybody had seen a Dogman. It sort of became like people have that on the brain."

Joedy Cook of the North American Dogman Project, when asked about the comparison between these two cryptids, mentions alleged Sasquatch reports he investigated in the 90s.

"I went back and looked at these reports, and the thing is… these people were seeing Dogmen. When you go back through some of these old reports, that's what it is. Now when people look at it today, they see what they think might be a Bigfoot or might be a Dogman, but the way I look at it, Dogman is not a big, burly, muscular animal. He's more of a thinner animal, he's taller. He does have muscles, but he's not built like an ape. More built like a dog standing up. That, to me, is what is confusing right now, because it depends on how the person interprets the sighting."

The Bear King of Marble Falls

There is one case in Texas, in the very heart of the Texas Dogman Triangle, which seems to split the difference between Sasquatch-like behavior and a canine appearance, known as the Bear King of Marble Falls.

This narrative nearly fits the motif of many "damsel-in-distress" style fairy tales, but with an interesting twist: the "damsel" in question rescues herself.

The story goes that a particularly lovely young woman named Arlen, a resident of the area now known as Marble Falls, was out one day in the Texas wilderness seeing to her daily chores. Without warning, she was swept off her feet (in a very unromantic sense), kidnapped, and dragged off into the hills without a trace. Arlen's mother, who was in the nearby family cabin, reported hearing not only her daughter shouting for help, but also bestial, terrifying howls or screams from some unseen animal.

When word of her disappearance spread a posse was formed. The locals took up arms and set off in search of the young woman, prowling the hills and valleys *en masse* until dark.

They found nothing.

Traversing the Texas Hill Country at night without a reliable light source is a surefire way to sustain an injury or fall to one's death. Even with the aid of a modern flashlight this is a dangerous venture, and the townspeople very likely lacked that luxury. The next morning the search was resumed, and before long Arlen was found wandering aimlessly through the woods by one of the members of the party, apparently in a state of bewilderment.

As strange as this was, her account of her time absent from her family was even stranger. She told her rescuers - or finders, really, since no one had rescued her other than herself - that a large, hairy, two-legged creature had emerged from the woods, thrown her over its shoulder and stalked off into the brush. She described it as being bear-like in appearance, with shaggy brown fur and a grumpy disposition, towering no less than seven-feet-tall.

The fiend took her to a place locally known as the Moon Mountains, where she was kept captive through the night. Her assailant didn't harm her but would also not allow her to leave its lair. She eventually managed to slip away, perhaps when her savage abductor went to sleep or left in search of food.

Naturally, the locals were incensed. To simply hope the thing would not come back was by no means an option. They once more took up arms and headed straight for the Moon Mountains, following the directions the girl had given them. When they came to the cave she described, they were confronted by a monstrous figure. The descriptions are vague but seem to equate to a cross between a canine, bear, and primate. Pointed ears, sharp fangs, angry eyes, and thick fur. Tall. Muscular. Terrifying.

The brute charged and howled at the townspeople. Whether it was intent on harm or intimidation is not known, but it is irrelevant. The posse immediately opened fire. The beast succumbed to a hail of lead.

Supposedly, a local group of Native Americans were believed to have a story in their oral history called "The Bear King." This has not been confirmed, and assumptions cannot be made concerning Native American lore without proper cultural knowledge. Regardless of its origin, the name stuck. To date The Bear King of Marble Falls is the moniker assigned to the tale. One important thing to note is that there are no "Moon Mountains" in Marble Falls.

There is, however, a peak with an elevation of just over 370 meters called Moon Mountain, located a little over forty miles south of modern-day Marble Falls (60-70 miles by car). Interestingly enough, Moon Mountain is accessible only by traversing a side road connected to a highway known locally as The Devil's Backbone.

The Devil's Backbone is a limestone ridge where a vicious battle is said to have taken place during the Civil War. Locals and travelers purport that the ghosts of the fallen Confederate and Union soldiers remain and can be seen on a regular basis. It may be that this Moon Mountain is the same one mentioned in the story, but additional details have proven elusive. It remains yet another odd feature of the Hill Country cloistered around other folklore and paranormally adjacent tales.

The topography of both Marble Falls and the Moon Mountain peak are riddled with limestone bluffs and interconnected caves, so at least this element of the story seems plausible. In the late 1800s, when the story is said to have occurred, there would have been significantly less development than there is today. In other words, there would have been more wild country to be a refuge for an aberrant beast.

Marble Falls is incidentally only 38 miles by car from Lake Travis and connected to that strange area by the Colorado River. In a straight line, they are merely 22 miles apart. Perhaps the towering bipedal figure captured on camera at Lake Travis in 2007 (see: Chapter 1) has some connection to the fabled Bear King?

This story is detailed on numerous websites, but the version given here was relayed by Michael Mayes of *Texas Cryptid Hunter*.

All this to say that Dogman and Sasquatch are inexplicably linked, and opinions on the nature of that link are varied. The consensus seems to bounce between two conclusions: they may be the same thing, or they may be entirely separate things. There are certainly enough stories which straddle the line to make either argument. This exploration, however, is not meant to center on Sasquatch, and thus we will return to talking of wolves.

4

When We Say Dogman

There is a question to ask before we proceed further: *What is Dogman?*

This is not a simple question. On the surface it is a wolf, or dog, which can walk upright without the aid of its forelimbs on the ground. Cynocephalus is an older term for the creature but means much the same thing. Some would say "monster," others "animal," and others still "nonsense." The question becomes more complicated when we attempt to define the origin and nature of these beings. Given the many available sources of information, the time periods in which the archetype is found, and the variety of cultures which have perpetuated the myths, there really may be no concrete answer.

I've been asked this many times in recent months - what do you think Dogman is? In truth, no hard conclusion seems satisfactory yet. Encounters with these beings run the gamut from simply seeing a strange dog to the highly supernatural. There is talk of them being affiliated with UFO sightings, perhaps hinting at the supposition that they may be extraterrestrial in origin. The stories of werewolves from old Europe would cast them as malevolent shapeshifters, while those attempting to apply more "hard science" to the question might lean towards what Linda Godfrey coined as an "Indigenous Dogman." Most witnesses describe a sense of overwhelming fear, while some mention literal physical paralysis. There are stories of witnesses experiencing telepathic communication when face to face with an upright canid, and even tales of them donning body armor and engaging in firefights with the US military.

With any inquiry into the unsolved, it is prudent to consider as many opinions as possible and pieces of evidence which can be gathered (within reason). When it comes to the question of Dogman, the variety of stories associated with this phenomenon lend it to myriad interpretations. As such, I asked several of my fellow researchers and enthusiasts for their perspective. So, through the opinions and experiences of other researchers, let us dive into the query: *What is Dogman?*

Jessi and Joe Doyle of Hellbent Holler offered this:

"We know that the phenomenon is real. We just don't know what it is yet. We have had experiences with something while at The Land Between the Lakes that matched up exactly with several witness accounts. What we encountered during our first sighting was physical, evidenced by marks left on the environment and heat signatures captured on thermal imaging equipment. However, our second and third encounters were with something that seemed physical for a few seconds, but then just seemed to fade away. Both the material and the immaterial sightings took place within a mile from one another in the northern end of the LBL, just a stone's throw away from the location of the alleged 1980's RV massacre."[7]

Ashley Hilt is the co-host of *On Wednesdays, We Talk Weird,* a popular podcast specializing in the strange and unsolved. She is also a Fortean investigator who has invested years into researching, among many dozens of other things, the Mothman phenomena, and is currently producing a documentary film titled *Synching the*

---

[7] Please note: Readers are encouraged to keep careful watch on the Hellbent Holler team. Their explorations of The Land Between the Lakes documented in their series of videos titled *The Werewolf Experiments* are available for free on Youtube, and to research this phenomenon without examining their work is folly. This is also not the only topic which Jessi and Joe have investigated, and hours may be spent reviewing their catalog of work.

Mothman. I posited the same question to her that I submitted to Jessi and Joe.

"In my research, I am pretty confident that the entire phenomenon is supernatural. Whether these creatures actually look like buff, tall, bipedal canines or they just present themselves that way so that the experiencer KNOWS they're experiencing something strange, I can't say. However, after studying the logistics of what a prehistoric canine might evolve into, bipedal does not make much sense. Not only that, but there seems to be a lot of fear associated with these things. While coming across any wild animal is scary, there doesn't seem to be the same reaction that you get with something like Bigfoot."

The significance of the evolutionary possibility of these animals is a common argument against their existence. I asked Courteney Swihart, a Registered Veterinary Technician with thirteen years of experience in the field for her opinion. She specializes in neurology and has a degree in veterinary medicine. For those not aware, a RVT (or LVT, CVT, RVN or any number of other acronyms depending upon the state in question) is the veterinary equivalent of a Registered Nurse. They are required to hold a degree, pass a state board exam, and administer the same treatments with the same expertise as a veterinarian. Her remarks on the topic provide a valuable perspective. When I inquired after the possibility of an unidentified dog-wolf breed in Texas, she said this,

"Canine 'breeds' are constantly evolving. Both on their own, mating in the wild, and humans trying to make a new looking dog. I have no doubt if you look hard enough you can find a dog that looks differently than we would expect, however, to be a *breed* of dog that would imply a large enough number for them to have a breeding population, which would maybe lower the odds. Also note that some hybrids are infertile due to their genetics, which would also limit some of the weirder mixes."

I also asked Courteney for any examples she may be aware of involving dogs either walking on their rear legs or using their front legs in a bizarre or unusual manner. Relevant examples might provide an answer to at least some Dogman-type sightings.

"I have seen dogs who were born with only two legs or lost legs due to trauma walk upright, even run. They usually develop arthritis at a young age due to extra stress on their joints, but they can get around great."

She continued,

"Working in neurology I have seen some wild things. I have seen dogs and cats compensate for being paralyzed in amazing ways. Also, very sick animals, such as with encephalitis or brain injury, can do some incredibly bizarre things. I have seen several patients with severe encephalitis look like they are dancing for hours, which can be considered seizures, but to someone who didn't know it looks like they are jamming out."

This opens the possibility of additional misidentification. Not only might Sasquatch be mistaken for Dogman, but so might an ordinary dog. We cannot discount this possibility, even though many of the eyewitness testimonies to follow will make this explanation a difficult one to apply overall.

For our purposes, and for the duration of this volume, no hard stance will be taken on the nature of these supposed canines. Indefinite time might be spent discussing the meaning of the "paranormal" as it relates to sightings of unidentified animals, and to come down conclusively on any one notion would be to omit the others without sufficient data. Some explanations are more outlandish than others, but all require at least a small leap of faith.

Granted, most of the encounters in this book are approached from the perspective of an organic creature which is yet to be scientifically classified, but that is not to say that any explanation is off the table. For example, there is research to support an extraterrestrial hypothesis, including some of the work done by Jessi and Joe Doyle. Another particularly entertaining theory (which has also been applied to Sasquatch) is that of a portal-jumping horror from another dimension. Some have speculated that they may be the result of a government experiment either gone wrong or were intended to be bad news from the outset. Either way, this line of thinking states that the beasts are genetically manufactured. Still others believe the phenomenon is supernatural and that these are malignant entities purely spiritual in makeup. Sightings near graveyards might lend some credence to this idea, but then we must speculate on the nature of ghosts, hauntings, and the spirit realm - and we simply do not have the time!

The encounters in this book contain many overlapping features, but the supernatural, spiritual, extraterrestrial element is not largely seen. The Texan Dogman behaves - mostly - like an animal, and our discussion will take its tone with this in mind. That said, readers are encouraged to keep an eye out for patterns in these various accounts, particularly in relation to the behavior and appearance of the entities themselves and the human experiencers who encounter them.

The terms Dogman and werewolf will also be used interchangeably, and this is done for two reasons. One, to help prevent the language of the manuscript from becoming stale, as the word "Dogman" already appears over 150 times within the text. Two, and perhaps more importantly, both terms are consistent with what the witnesses herein describe. The term "Wolfman" is also in the mix but does not often appear in eyewitness testimony. We will not posit that the things referred to as "werewolves" transform under a full moon from a normal human to a bloodthirsty fiend. This is, by and large, accepted as a Hollywood invention, drawn from traces of old European werewolf lore and with little to no foundation in reality.

When we say Dogman, we are referring to the phenomena of witnesses describing an upright-walking wolf or dog. A cynocephalus. A human/dog mixture. They may be spiritual. They may be physical - in many cases leaving hard evidence. They may be something else entirely around which we have yet to wrap our collective mind. Whatever they are, my research into the various cases in this book, as well as many hours of conversation with other Fortean researchers, has convinced me of one certainty:

Werewolves exist, and they live in Texas.

The Texas Dogman Triangle

Until now, most of our exploration has been focused outside the primary topic of this volume. This has been done to set the stage, in hopes that by examining a few (of many) facets of Texan high strangeness, the reader may more fully appreciate the background of surrounding accounts of upright canines. John Keel postulated that all paranormal phenomena are interconnected, projected into our world by something he called the Super Spectrum, detailed in his essential work *The Eighth Tower*. Other paranormal scribes have speculated along similar lines, though few have taken as hard of a stance as Keel. Whether or not this is an accurate assessment is another topic entirely; but, if it holds water, the surrounding strangeness in the state may have direct or indirect correlation to encounters with animals we refer to as Dogman.

Designation of the "Texas Dogman Triangle" came about by cross referencing reports and historical cases from a variety of sources, including eyewitnesses, written accounts both in print and online, and, in part, by noting certain geographical locations which seem to indicate the presence of wolves or wolf-adjacent animals. While potential Dogman encounters can be found across the state, the Triangle presents both a crossover of historical and modern anecdotes, as well as repeated and strikingly close proximity to areas of other concentrated high strangeness.

My initial interest in this area began in 2021 while doing research for an episode of *Hey Strangeness*, a podcast I co-host with my wife, Sara. We focused on three potential Dogman encounters adjacent to Lake Travis, a place which had already made its way onto my radar due to the myriad odd occurrences reported there. Placed on a map, these encounters encompass an area of 700 square miles. This is a wide region of space, spread across undeveloped and largely unexplored wildlands. There are nature preserves, miles of creeks, and scores of limestone caves and bluffs. There are plenty of towns and cities, thickest at this early triangle's corners, but most of this vast area consists of untouched wilderness. Outside of the main housing areas, there are many farms and ranches, lakes, rivers, forests, plains, and so on. The ideal environment for a predatory animal, and an easy place in which to get lost. The feasibility of an undiscovered species in this region "dogged" me.

This was the beginning of the Texas Dogman Triangle and served as the initial anchor point from which later sightings were mapped. After production of the podcast had wrapped, I continued to research Texan werewolves with casual interest. I soon realized that I had set the borders of the Triangle too close together. It was, quite simply, too small. We had grossly under-represented the scope of this idea in our show. It was only the beginning.

As the triangle expanded, these three encounters were moved from the three corners to a cluster somewhere near the middle. In keeping with the paranormal enthusiast's habit of assigning arbitrary names to what we like to call window areas, this section was labeled as the Wolf Mountain Cluster.

Now that we have covered the origin and beginning stages of my ever-evolving research journey, we are ready to get down to specifics. So, without further ado, let's enter the Triangle.

5

The Wolf Mountain Cluster - Lampasas, Austin, Johnson City, Fredericksburg – 2016, 2018, 2020

There is a vast, rolling swathe of Hill Country north of San Antonio and just south of Austin. Many small and burgeoning communities are scattered throughout this region with folklore and legends both modern and historical. Like most parts of the state, there is a wealth of history here intermixed with plenty of strange accounts and bizarre phenomena.

The territory in question runs near storied San Antonio, parallel to the state capitol of Austin and is a gateway to hundreds of miles of plains, forests, rivers, desert, swamps, and more (it also includes Lake Travis). There are plenty of towns beyond this "western gateway," but they are spread far and often thin across the sprawling landscape. Massive parcels of ranch land take up much of this space, and road hypnosis is not an uncommon affliction. As stated, much of the region is undeveloped. There is beyond abundant space to conceal ruined farmhouses and the ancient husks of rusted agricultural equipment. There is an old-world feel to this area once you leave the more populated centers of San Antonio, Austin, San Marcos, and New Braunfels, and enter the territory dubbed regionally as the Texas Hill Country.

One gets a sense of history passing through the less traveled byways. New and old structures are stacked side-by-side, surrounded by dozens of State Historical Markers and small-town main streets. It is just as likely that a passerby will see a rancher on horseback or a real-life Longhorn as it is that they may see another motorized vehicle on the scenic back route from Austin to San Antonio along US Highway 281. Cattle, goats, and chickens are common, along with the other assorted fauna of the Hill Country.

Here, in the still growing, old-meets-new of Central Texas a sequence of odd sightings has taken place. They begin (as far as we know) in 2016 and can be accounted for as recently as 2020. Each taken on their own may be written off as a fluke, a hallucination, or a misidentification - and - in truth, these reports may be just that. But when taken together and examined in sequence, a distinct and difficult to ignore pattern begins to emerge. An image takes the shape of long-forgotten monsters lurking in the thickets and scrublands. Depictions that whisper of pointed teeth, savage claws, and creatures dredged straight from the primordial nightmares of our ancient ancestors.

Near Lampasas, Texas - 2018

"It just looked like a beast."

Trent Fulton has an impressive resume. It's the sort that employers will fight over in the 21st century, particularly in an era where labor is in short supply and qualified candidates can be equated to water in the desert.

He holds a degree in sports management from NYU Business School. He is a veteran of the National Guard and served two combat tours during the conflict in Afghanistan. He is the father of two intelligent, thriving, and well-adjusted children, and at writing has nearly completed putting them both through school. He is an entrepreneur and holds real estate licenses in Texas and Colorado. If time is money, Trent's time is cryptocurrency backed by precious metals insured by the FDIC and buried in a treasure chest off an unknown coast.

In 2018 Trent was on the road, driving with his wife and sons from Denver, CO to Austin, TX on a summer visit to spend time with family. Trent is accustomed to long drives. Previous treks have included Nebraska to Texas, Texas to New York, New York to Arizona, Arizona to Colorado, and on and on and on. He prefers to be the driver - let the family sleep, focus on the road, and ensure a safe arrival. It's something he's good at and has described the source of his ability to commute the endless expanses of the US highway system simply and honestly as "adrenaline." His father, after all, has worked as a long-haul trucker for decades. Perhaps it's in his blood.

But, on August 15th of 2018 something changed. What had previously been an uneventful drive - Trent had made the journey before, and more than once – became an encounter out of step with his prior road trips. Something that would burrow itself into his mind indefinitely, nagging at him in the wee hours of the morning, in moments of silence, and oddly, during the occasional streaming horror movie.

US Highway 183 connects Lampasas and Austin, TX. Like most cities in the state, Lampasas has its share of ghost stories and folk tales. The highway runs through the hill country over wide bends and wooded straights. Like other rural Texas routes there are untold reaches of hills, plains, and forest surrounding portions of 183 from all directions. Wildlife is not an uncommon sight on these back roads, and even main highways see their share of deer, raccoons, and many other critters.

Trent describes an upright animal, crouched on two hind legs. Its ears pointed upwards, in a fashion that reminded him of a purebred canine. Animal eyes flashed in the LED headlights, and beneath them a set of wicked, almost too-long teeth smeared with what Trent assumed to be blood. Hooked claws were tearing at a fleshy wad of gore - a deer carcass - and the frame of the creature was both slender and muscular. Trent locked eyes with the thing for the briefest of moments. *Should he slow down and try to get a better look, or even turn around and go back?*

It was approximately 11 PM. This stretch of road is extremely rural, and the headlights of the Mercedes-Benz GLE-Class were the only source illumination, save a few stray stars and a dim glow from the waning gibbous moon. The weather was clear, with average temperatures that time of year running between 46 and 59 degrees. Clouds and fog were nearly non-existent, and visibility could easily be described as decent to excellent. If he had stopped, there would be little to obstruct his view...

...and little to obstruct the creature's view of him. Nothing to hide behind, seek shelter within or otherwise escape to, should the need arise. Except, of course, the Mercedes GLE-Class.

His family was in the car, and with no buildings or other vehicles in sight, the potential to be in a dangerous situation without immediate help was very real. Trent has been in dangerous situations before and knows better than to wander into them unnecessarily.

He kept driving.

The experience became a much-forgotten footnote in his colorful past, until one day a friend casually mentioned over drinks that they've been getting into sightings of "real werewolves." I was that friend, and after a moment of surprised silence Trent said, "Well, I saw something once." We discussed the matter at length, and later set up a proper interview to dissect Trent's sighting.

"Imagine a big, muscular dog with an ungodly face. When the headlights caught it and we locked eyes, you could just see the mouth of fangs and sharp teeth. Had black death eyes. It was a rounder head, almost like a huge Razor Edge Pitbull. That's the best reference I had, but it wasn't a pit. It was taller. Just scary looking. It was crouched over a dead deer."[8]

---

[8] The Razor Edge Pitbull is a sub-breed of the American Staffordshire Terrier. They have bulkier shoulders than some of their cousins due to a mix of English Bulldog DNA in their lineage.

As he passed the creature at approximately fifty-five miles per hour, Trent swore he saw it stand up.

On two legs.

Trent expressed regret at not turning back for a better look, but one can hardly blame him. Risking an encounter with a wild, potentially dangerous, beast in the middle of the night in the middle of nowhere with one's wife and family is hardly advisable.

This is an interesting story, made even more interesting by the credibility of the witness. Without financial incentive, a desire for fame or a predilection towards falsehood, it seems odd that a "normal" person would relay such a tale for fear of being ridiculed. Indeed, Trent Fulton is a pseudonym - while the witness stands by the story and has changed not a single detail over multiple retellings, they have no desire for public recognition. I found the tale convincing, both due to my relationship to the witness which breeds an inclination towards trust, and the consistencies between this story and similar encounters with creatures of almost identical descriptions.

Perhaps it is easier to believe a story relayed by someone you know and trust than by a stranger or a web posting. But random stories from anonymous internet users can have value, and in the case of Trent's sighting, would only add fuel to a rapidly expanding fire.

The North American Dogman Project, headed by Joedy Cook, has one of the most comprehensive libraries of Dogman evidence, encounters, and folklore on the web. One can easily lose half an afternoon to delving through the NADP archives. Early in my research I found the NADP website an interesting and invaluable research tool and had been fortunate to correspond with Joedy on numerous occasions on the topic of strange canid encounters. Joedy comes from a background of military and law enforcement and approaches his investigations through the practiced lens of his training and experience. One particularly interesting feature of the website is the *Encounters* map; an interactive Google map with an index of eye-witness encounters spanning the globe. Each sighting is reported independently to the NADP, reviewed by the team, and then shared as a part of the database. If Fulton's encounter provided the foundation of the Texas Dogman Triangle, the NADP website provided the cornerstone.

Fredericksburg, Johnson City, and Lampasas are the closest population centers to the Fulton encounter and the two corroborating encounters on the NADP website.

Near Fredericksburg - 2020

To the west, the city of Fredericksburg has the honor of being the first German town in Texas. 100-year-plus-old structures characterize the historic community, and what was once an undiscovered jewel of quaint Lone Star charm now boasts property values exceeding ten million dollars and then some. If one is skeptical of this claim, one need only consult the internet. Inflating property values in Texas have been on the rise for at least ten years, but in recent times they have subverted the expectations of even the most venerable experts.

In 2020 an anonymous witness described an encounter strikingly like Mr. Fulton's - passing a large, bipedal canine-like beast kneeling by the side of the road at night. This encounter listed a witness in addition to the driver, who initially dubs the creature "Dogman" and urges the driver to speed up and keep going.

The witness was driving on June 27, 2020, much like Trent in the preceding story, towards Austin from out of state in their trusty pick-up truck. They were traveling with their daughter and 6-year-old granddaughter, likely quite weary after making the trek from California.

From the NADP website:

"I had taken 290 east off I-10 and it was around 11pm. We had gone a few miles on 290 when coming up over a hill and looking down at the bottom of the hill I picked up a pair of yellow almond shaped eyes off to the right. This part of 290 is fairly remote and heavily wooded with scrub oak and there were no other vehicles on the road. The deer population here in the hill country of Texas is huge and I was being extremely vigilant because I had already passed a number of deer grazing along the roadside."

This is a verifiable detail. I have personally driven this same stretch of highway many, many times and experienced the same (regarding the deer). For a considerable time, Sara and I lived off Highway 290 in South Austin. Driving west along this route out of the city proper takes one into a region which is every bit Texas Hill Country, and it is inundated with whitetail deer.

"As we got closer my headlights revealed a large, and what I thought at first was a wolf; however, it wasn't a wolf or coyote. It was on all fours and in a crouched defensive posture about 20 feet off the roadside. It had its head down and its front legs were bent, but it was still taller at the shoulders (3 to 4 feet) than its rear. It had a triangular head with pointed ears and a short tail."

This witness's description is not unlike Trent's. Pointed ears and a fixating gaze, though Trent described the subject of his sighting near Lampasas as having "death black" eyes, not yellow. The witness continues,

"It was broad across the shoulders with narrow hips, and a long neck. The coat on this creature was heavy/bushy below the neck, on the front legs and tapered off towards the rear with the short tail being bushy. The front legs looked very muscular and the feet were not real distinct because of the grass. It never took its eyes off us as we went past and it maintained the same posture, which I thought was unusual because I expected it to turn and run back into the tree line."

The witness was unsure what to think of the thing, but one of the passengers provided ample commentary.

"My Daughter got the best look at this thing as we went by. My Daughter quickly informed me that it was not a coyote or wolf, and to not stop and keep driving because she said it was a Dogman, which I had really never heard a lot about. This is the most perplexing wildlife encounter I have ever had. I grew up in Texas and have deer hunted all over the state when I was younger. I moved to California for 17 years and lived adjacent to the Cleveland National Forest, where I saw an abundance of coyotes, bobcats and on one occasion a close encounter with a cougar. This made my hairs stand up on my arms as we got down the road. I will never forget it."

The NADP Encounters map lists this location as being close to Fredericksburg, Texas. Fredericksburg is a wonder, and this association with a werewolf-like entity could not be overlooked. If this was the only anecdote to come out of Fredericksburg it would still be worth mentioning, but a comment posted on the article *Dogman Encounter in Kerrville, TX* on the *True Horror Stories of Texas* website by a user identified as Dan Waters provides an interesting correlation.

Waters purports that in 2020 he encountered strange tracks on his ranch in the Fredericksburg area like those mentioned in other Dogman encounters. He had also seen similar tracks 18 years before. An attempt was made to contact Waters for a more in-depth interview, but this was sadly not possible. Nevertheless, the sheer happenstance of finding a website independent of the NADP that contained this correlating piece of anecdotal evidence outlining activity in the same area of Texas gives one pause.

Near Johnson City (Pedernales Falls State Park) - 2016

Johnson City, so named for President Lyndon Johnson, is the birthplace of the former president, and his childhood home stands there to this day. The city plays host to an annual holiday light display which can be seen from space (according to NASA) and is nestled in the rural stretches of an otherwise undeveloped expanse of territory.

The third - or perhaps fourth, as the prints mentioned by Mr. Waters did not come to my notice until very recently - anecdote out of the Wolf Mountain Cluster comes from around Pedernales Falls State Park near Johnson City, which is one of the larger population centers near the park.

This witness decided to camp for the evening on "*a private ranch near Pedernales State Park,*" and their story may require a tad more suspension of disbelief than those we've examined so far. The witness described horrible, savage howling noises coming from the woods which they at first attributed to rowdy campers but later concluded could not be coming from any human or animal with which they are familiar.

The witness was given free reign of the private land, encouraged to explore, and set up camp wherever they wished. They chose the most isolated spot available, settling on a location near the very edge of the property line. This was situated closest to the wilderness and near a creek atop a ridge that overlooked a valley. The witness described screams, both during and after setting up camp. The yells seemed to come from three to four people, with two voices that were distinctly male in tone and at least one which the witness identified as female.

The evening continued, as did the screaming, and the witness occupied themself by gathering firewood. They estimated that the source of the noise was approximately

150 meters below the campsite, down the ridge and closer to the creek.

Again, from the NADP website:

"After attending a matter in Austin during the day, I decided to camp out near Pedernales Falls State Park in a private ranch that I won't name (lady there was really nice and don't wish her any bad business). It was after dark-- about 6:30 pm last Friday, November 18, 2016, when I was invited to explore and set up camp anywhere on the property. I went to the most isolated part in the back near a creek.

"Once in the area, I heard screams made by people-- approximately two males and one or two females. At first, I thought to myself 'Damn, I'm going to have to hear these drunks yell all night as they blast off their primal scream therapy routine.' They had set a campfire below next to the creek. I was about 150 yards away, high up near the ledge. The creek ran about 10 yards below me and I caught a glimpse of their fire but not of the people. Only quick shadows darted past the flames. It was odd but I did not think much of it at the time.

"I proceeded to return to my area where I'd parked my car and gathered firewood. I ignored the screams that these folks were making... yet I noticed that I never once heard talking or voices commenting in normal language.... just screams that kept getting more intense and strong and long (in duration). Still, I did not think of it as being too weird. I kept about my business trying to set up my camp and my tent in the dark.

"After struggling, flashlight in my mouth, and knees scraped from laying out the bedding in the tent, I walked around enjoying the open view of the sky. By now, the screams had turned to barking and howling.

"Earlier during my wood gathering forage I had heard someone walking in the darkness and I assumed it to be a person who probably had strayed from their perimeter to go to the bathroom. I spoke to the person in the dark mentioning that I would be setting up camp in this upper area away from them. The person never answered so I felt confident I had established a respectful territorial mark where I would not go near them and they, in turn, would not come close to me. Nevertheless, I still did not think anything was weird up to that point. What began to worry me was when an hour later, as I was about to begin my fire, and rest in my tent, three or four howls united into a very loud crescendo. That got my attention. The barking now was more intense and deeper. At first, I thought that maybe these people were using dogs to fight each other but it was not like that. In dog fights you can listen to dogs tearing into each other and the voices of the men cheering on.

"Here, the barking seemed to be going in one direction, as if the dogs or coyotes were competing to outdo each other with barks, wailing, and howling. As my mind tried to comprehend what was going on another possible scenario appeared to my reasoning capability--maybe they had set up speakers and were playing a recording of barks and howls... but it made no sense. Once again, the barking deepened and the howling became more fierce and louder. That when [sic] I decided that I would not be able to sleep there at all; besides, the sounds did not appear to be human-based at all. I collapsed the tent I had struggled to set up (for almost an hour) and left the stone ring and all the firewood of different lengths and thickness stacked and ready.

"A sense of self-preservation came over me as I was alone, unarmed except for a long, heavy machete I gripped with my right hand. Before leaving I crept as far as I could to the ledge where earlier I had seen their campfire but the barking and howling was too great. I crept up quietly in defensive combat mode only 25 yards further (did not reach the 50 yard mark at the ledge where I'd been two hours earlier). How I wished to have my tape recorder box with batteries so that my wife could hear what I was hearing. Like I said, I could not go any deeper or closer to them because the things voicing out the barking and howls were not people.

"I never saw them."

It is an interesting, if minor, synchronicity that all three of the witnesses in these encounters were traveling to or from the city of Austin. That aside, there are a few problems with this one. First, the witness admits to never seeing the source of the noises. He also never claims to get a good look at the people he suspects are camping nearby, and his primary pieces of evidence are unidentified cries from an unknown beast of some sort.

In interviewing members of the veterinary community, and reviewing examples provided by them via video, one will come to learn that known animals are capable of making ghastly, unearthly, terrifying noises. In our discussion of this case, my wife Sara (a veterinary technician with ten years of experience) showed me a video of a dog in a kennel being prepared for a surgical procedure. The dog was in distress and making a sound which immediately made me think of monsters and demons from the great beyond. It was unnerving, even seeing the source. A guttural, snarling, high pitched yet strangely rhythmic sound falling somewhere between a growl and a child crying.

"This can't be a normal dog."

"It is," Sara said with a straight face, "they do this all the time."

On the other hand, to discount the word of someone familiar with spending time in the wilderness - the witness's comfort in the woods is implied by the fact that they were camping alone - would be a hasty mistake. There is something to be said for the opinion of someone accustomed to the sounds of the natural world, and it is worth noting when such an individual points out a deviation. By the same token, to disregard correlating evidence provided by a veterinary professional would be equal in hubris.

The question must be asked, however, that if these sounds were produced by ordinary coyotes or something similar, what caused them to go into such a frenzy that a seasoned outdoorsman chose to abandon his campsite in the middle of the night?

Pedernales Falls State Park is significant to the makeup of the Texas Dogman Triangle both for its location and for an interestingly named geographical feature within its bounds - Wolf Mountain. No direct link to werewolf mythology has yet been found to exist and the origin of the name is yet a mystery. Attempts to contact a representative of Pedernales Falls State Park resulted in the following reply through a private Facebook message,

"We could not find anything special about the naming of Wolf Mountain. Likely it was named that by previous owners of the land, or by the first park rangers who were naming trails and landmarks to help visitors navigate. There have been populations of Prairie wolves in Texas before, and sometimes coyotes were nicknamed prairie wolves by settlers in the area. Today there are still coyotes but no known wolves here at the park."

Given that Texas has been home to Mexican Red Wolves, Gray Wolves, Dire Wolves, coyotes, and strange canid hybrids (as previously examined), it is not surprising that more than one geographical feature would be so named. There are many such locations: additional Wolf Mountains, Wolf Creeks, Wolf Hills, etc.

The terrain of Wolf Mountain Trail within Pedernales State Park is a sprawling loop of nearly six miles. It is a rugged trek of changing elevations, thick vegetation, and low-lying waterways. The Pedernales River both borders and divides the park at its northern and eastern ends, irrigating the forest and connecting it to more northern stretches of the countryside (including the Lake Travis). Like other parts of the Wolf Mountain Cluster and the Texas Dogman Triangle as a whole, it provides the ideal environment for an animal that wishes to remain concealed. The park is home to abundant whitetail deer, as well as raccoons, rabbits, armadillos, and other staples of Hill Country wildlife. Overall, it consists of over 5,000 acres, and this does not account for the stretches of wilderness which surround it and roll well beyond its perimeter.

As I write this, a planned trip to Pedernales Falls State Park to take pictures, poke around and "investigate" has been indefinitely postponed. As mentioned earlier, wildfires are a part of the Texas ecology, and currently the park is closed for just that reason. 115 individual fires, taking place within 83 counties and comprising over 10,000 acres, are currently ravaging the Hill Country in the heart of the Triangle. Despite this, there remains an untold wealth of hidden and unexplored places. One must hope that the blaze is brought under swift control, for the sake of both the wildlife and the Hill Country's human residents.

In summary, what we have is an almost unthinkable amount of space which is unobserved by human beings the great majority of the time. With so many protected areas including state parks and recharge zones for the Edwards Aquifer, urbanization of these spaces moves at a slower pace than some other parts of Texas. On top of that, much of the land is privately owned by ranchers, proprietors of breweries and wineries, and farmers. Here we see immense parcels of rural land, more developed than the wild country around them, but still vast enough to provide ample opportunity for concealment to crafty, exotic fauna.

Moving west, away from the Wolf Mountain Cluster, we find a much older story. This tale cannot be corroborated by contemporary witnesses, but it is a strange legacy set in stone. Literally.

6

The Beast of Bear Creek - Cleo, Texas – 1800's

Here, far west of San Antonio and greatly removed from the hustle and bustle of the metropolitan wards of the Lone Star State, we find the most southwestern point of the Texas Dogman Triangle. It lies deep in the rural stretches of West Texas, but still is well away from the border of New Mexico. This is an old story - so old in fact, that the town associated with the tale no longer exists, and researching it presents unique challenges.

Cleo, Texas was founded in 1860. Originally it was called Viejo and was renamed Cleo in 1920 after the local postmaster's niece, when it was discovered that another *Viejo, Texas* already existed. The closest large population center is Junction, Texas - so named as it is the junction of two major branches of the North and South Llano Rivers. In addition, it serves as the county seat of Kimble County, and today holds a population of just over 2,600.

As of the year 2000, Cleo was a ghost town; the census that year listed the population as *three*. As such, locating a primary source for this story has proven impossible, even after several months of dedicated searching. All that remains of the Beast of Bear Creek is a folk tale, and a strange face carved into the side of a limestone bluff. The closest we can get in 2022 - as far as we know - is to hear the tale from those who remember it.

The Story of the "Shaman"

Fortunately, Michael Mayes is one such individual. Michael, who we met in an earlier chapter, is a long-time researcher, educator, and respected author. There are few others alive today who can tell the story of Cleo without having to look it up on the internet first, and those who do endeavor to search for the tale will inevitably find Michael's article on the *Texas Cryptid Hunter* website. This was my first exposure to the Bear Creek saga, and I was eager to interview Michael as one of the rare individuals who could recount it.

The Beast of Bear Creek has been in Michael's orbit for most of his life. Michael was a boy scout and is no stranger to the woods of the Hill Country: "I grew up in Texas, so campfire stories... I've heard a lot of stuff."

The story purports that a Native American shaman, perhaps the last of his tribe, sought vengeance on the white settlers of Kimble County for atrocities committed against his people.[9] He would transform into a savage beast - an upright walking wolf, much in the vein of traditional Skinwalker legends - and woe be to anyone unfortunate enough to cross paths with him.

The plan seemed relatively straightforward. The second aspect of this story, however, is a stark contrast to the metaphysical nature of the first.

N.Q. Patterson and the Cleo Face

N.Q. Patterson was a person of renown in Cleo back when it was a thriving community. He held many titles: county judge, county treasurer, and former law man, among others. At one time, he made a trip to Marfa, Texas - another hub of strangeness in the state - in pursuit of a group of bandidos.[10]

---

[9] Whether these horrid acts were perpetrated through physical violence, forced relocation, or the spreading of disease is unknown: however, any comparable scenario certainly provides sufficient incentive for revenge.
[10] Like many characters associated with the legends in this book, we could spend an indefinite amount of time recalling the interesting facets of Mr. Patterson's life.

Patterson was, by most accounts, the person commissioned to chisel headstones for the recently deceased in Kimble County.

Michael Mayes recalls:

"Apparently he had a bit of an artistic bent, and he didn't get it all out of his system through carving tombstones... so he took to carving things into the side of these cliff and bluff faces that littered the hill country. Limestone probably, is what most of them are, which explains why they weathered so easily. But among those was one that became known as the Cleo Face."

It is alleged that Patterson was familiar with the story of the Bear Creek monster and created the Cleo Face to represent it. Perhaps he encountered it himself, or perhaps he heard about it from other locals. This detail is lost to time.

Michael explains that visiting the Cleo Face today is an ambition likely to go unfulfilled. The parcel on which the carving sits is now private property, and the current owners have little interest in allowing legend trippers onto their land. Because of this, images of The Cleo Face are difficult to come by. Fortunately, an award-winning journalist named Mike Cox, whose work Michael Mayes referenced in his own, captured a picture of the Face in 1969 for an N.Q. Patterson- centered article featured in the San Angelo Standard-Times.[11]

The article provides valuable additional information on the life of N.Q. Patterson and includes interviews with locals. With so little on record concerning the Cleo Face,

---

[11] The article was reprinted by the Texas Folklore Society in 1999 in a collection of obscure pieces called *Features and Fillers: Texas Journalists on Texas Folklore*. Today it is hosted on the Portal to Texas History with permission from The University of North Texas. The author encourages the reader to take time to seek out this invaluable resource.

the 1999 publication featuring the 1969 article is an invaluable resource.[12]

Sadly, the article makes no mention of werewolves, wolfmen, Skinwalkers, malicious shamans or otherwise. Rather, it details several interesting aspects of N.Q. Patterson's life, including his bent for stone carving, but it does not specify what the face is meant to symbolize. It may be for this reason that an exact line cannot be drawn from the Bear Creek Monster to the N.Q. Patterson's elusive Face, but it does not change the fact that this is the assumption which is often made.

Michael continues:

"Why he did it, he never said, or at least it was never recorded. But people started to believe that this was a representation of this werewolf, this shapeshifter that was terrorizing everybody. So, the theory was that he must have seen it, he must have known something about it."

The Cleo Face is perhaps the only piece of "hard" evidence connected to the story of the Bear Creek monster, and its association is a loose one. Descriptions of the face would seem to indicate a canine visage - a pronounced snout, fangs or tusks, a wide mouth, and what may be a pair of slatted eyes. The 1969 photograph bears a slight resemblance to the Lon Chaney, Jr. Wolfman of Universal Studios fame. There are other descriptions - vampire, goblin, orc, demon, grumpy man with large teeth - which might also be applicable. Like a limestone ink blot, the nature of the Cleo Face is left to the interpretation of the person looking at it. We are sadly bereft of anyone who can tell us conclusively what it is, why Patterson carved it, or if it has any relation to the Bear Creek monster.

---

[12] As such, it must be noted here that the author wishes to express his sincere thanks to Mike Cox, the San Angelo Times, The Texas Folklore Society, and The University of North Texas for taking the time to record this piece of history.

"You'd be hard pressed to find anybody who knows anything about that story these days. Probably has to do with the fact that nobody lives there anymore. It's not even a community. It's just a couple old, abandoned buildings and a few tracts of land and that's about it," Michael says.

Cleo is now one of 511+ ghost towns in Texas. Perhaps some enterprising lover of history and folklore will one day establish a destination or attraction in the Cleo vicinity, but for now, we are left only with the story.

It may surprise the reader to learn that there is yet another story of a bipedal wolf associated with a strange stone carving in the state. This one is quite a bit more modern. The original report came from a well-known paranormal author and investigator - a certain Nick Redfern, who I would meet shortly after the writing of this chapter. The parallels with the Cleo Monster are few. There is one coincidence, though, which will make us question everything we think we know so far about werewolves in Texas. We will examine this report in short order, but some additional context is first required. Without further delay…let's set the stage.

7

The Kerrville Encounter - Kerrville, Texas - 2002

Kerrville, Texas. This city is a particularly juicy slice of Texas history pie. Archaeological remains suggest that human beings have inhabited this sector of the Hill Country for over 10,000 years. First Nations peoples such as the Kiowa, Lipan Apache, and Comanche hunted here in ages past. Their longstanding presence in the region is evidenced by dozens of stone artifacts, including components of tools and weapons that have been found consistently throughout the area by both historians and archaeologists. H-E-B, arguably the most popular grocery retailer in the state, was founded in Kerrville in 1905 and today boasts over 420 locations.

March of the Camels

In 1854, a US army encampment near Kerrville known as Camp Verde was the home of an experimental military operation involving the use of camels as ground transport in the hot and arid southwest, all to the tune of $30,000 American Dollars.[13] Almost one hundred camels were brought by boat from Africa and marched the sixty-two miles from Kerrville to San Antonio. Imagine such a sight along the route which is now Interstate 10. The operation was purported to be successful, and the future of the program seemed bright. Apparently, the animals did well in the Hill Country, perhaps finding it a pleasant reprieve from the heat of their native Tunisia.

However, the Civil War brought the experiment to an abrupt end, and the camels in the possession of the US

---

[13] This would be a little over $1.1 million in today's currency.

Army were allegedly dispensed of in one of two ways: releasing them into the wild or selling them off to a circus. The offspring of these wayward camels could be seen both in the southwestern US and nearby Mexico for years after if one knew where to look. Whether there remain any scions of said camels in 2022 is unknown, but some sources do state that they "gradually perished." Perhaps an expedition in search of the descendants of these camels would make for an interesting future study.

Annually Kerrville hosts music and art festivals. In 2006, the 150th anniversary of the "Texas Camel Drive" was celebrated in the form of a parade featuring a reenactment of the old timey caravan. The display was complete with real camels and actors dressed in period garb.

A Haunted History

Top secret Civil War era black ops aside, Kerrville is also notoriously haunted. The Kerr County Courthouse, Old Camp Verde - the ghosts of the camels of 1854 are said to still attend the historical site - and Schriener University have been the source of rumors and ghost stories for decades. Given the wealth of history here, it is probably not a terribly startling revelation when one learns that there is also a rich table of supernatural folklore. It may also be the home of werewolves, dogmen, hybrid canids or supernatural-interdimensional-extraterrestrial beings of unknown origin which look at least somewhat dog-like, and that is the reason we have selected it as an area of study.

Another Strange Canine

An account reported to *True Horror Stories of Texas* - a resource which will soon become quite familiar to readers of this volume - tells of a plain-sight encounter at dusk. The witness reported the sighting to *True Horror Stories of Texas* in 2020, but states that the encounter took place "back around 20 years ago." For clarity's sake, this would place the time of the sighting somewhere near the dawn of the new millennium, when much of the world was caught up in the throes of Y2K Fever.

The witness, identified only by the Reddit handle DeaththeEternal, states that while visiting their great aunt and uncle "in the region around Kerrville," they decided to take the family pet - a dachshund - out for a walk at sunset, accompanied by the great uncle in question. Without warning, the forest fell silent. The native white noise of the Hill Country - birds, insects, the rustling of small fauna in the underbrush - vanished. The dachshund froze as well, and the witness reports that the animal's sight was locked on something up ahead.

"There was a creature loping through there, a dog-like thing about the size of a large Labrador-dachshund hybrid, save that on the creature's neck there was a head the size of a bear, and the thing was loping up and down and up and down in a way that fitted that kind of…. build. It looked hypnotic in a sense, and I was more terrified than I have ever been with anything else I ever saw. It gave me a visceral understanding of Lovecraft's idea that things that just look fundamentally wrong are terrifying precisely because the proportions do not fit."

An interpretation of a strange canine by Mike Garcia.

Reading into this encounter, I was immediately reminded of the concept of the uncanny valley. When the depiction of a human being is *too* realistic but still identifiable as artificial, it can elicit fear or a fight-or-flight response in many people. For example, a story has circulated on the internet for several years that early versions of the animated movie *Shrek* were horrifying to test audiences of young children, so the design was tempered to be less realistic and more cartoonish. The witness's equivocation of the specimen they witnessed with "Lovecraftian" horror would seem to track with other descriptions of not-quite-right canines, both inside and outside of the Triangle, as do their description of its movements.

"The head was so massive that it dragged the body down with it when it moved. It had a very fluid aspect to the motion at the same time, and that dissonance is what made it hypnotic. Also, not an easy thing to forget because it just looked... wrong. Head goes down, back limbs go up. Head goes up, upper body goes up with it. All in this fluid motion. To be as specific as I can get."

DeaththeEternal's description paints a picture of an animal not quite intended for the natural world as we understand it. Could this be another strange hybrid in the vein of the Texas Terror Dog or the Galveston Wolves? Perhaps one whose genetic deviations from the rest of their genus are not as well consolidated as those other two offshoots, leading to the awkward gait and oversized head? The creature is not described as aggressive though it was "powerfully built," with muscular, "stout" upper limbs. This is also consistent with potential sightings of Dogmen as reported by the paranormal community at large.

Later in my research, I would come across a similar description regarding the locomotion of a dog-like being. But this description would not be the verbal recollection of an incident 20 years past, or even supplied in the form of a sketch or drawing. This "other" animal with a similar gait would come in the form of a short, albeit compelling video clip accompanied by the testimony of one who has come to know these strange canines intimately. This encounter would take place hundreds of miles from Kerrville, far in the North of Texas, near the Dallas/Fort Worth Metroplex.

8

Somewhere near Dallas/Fort Worth - 2021 - 2022

At War with the Wolves

John asked that his full name and city of residence not be shared. While John is his given name and he lives close to the Dallas/Fort Worth Metroplex, to be any more specific might invite the potential for danger. I was introduced to John in spring of 2022 by Joedy Cook and have corresponded with him on a somewhat regular basis during my research. His concern for privacy is easy to summarize.

"I don't want a bunch of idiots coming out on the property trying to get themselves killed."

John is a seasoned outdoorsman. He owns and confidently oversees a hundred acres of Texas Hill Country on the outskirts of Dallas/Fort Worth. The DFW region is enormous and sprawling, made of both concrete jungle and untamed wilds, spaced by miles upon miles of snaking highways and winding back roads. There are many, many rural properties and population centers within a hundred or fewer miles of DFW, itself the home of a gallery of strange events. The cataclysm which spawned perhaps the best-known conspiracy theory in American history - the assassination of President John F. Kennedy - took place in Dealey Plaza, in the heart of downtown Dallas. Sasquatch sightings litter the map. Ghosts inhabit untold dozens of historical buildings. Numerous books have been written on the anomalies of the Metroplex, and there is a wealth of available cases to dive into, including those in the cryptozoology niche. Until recently, stories of werewolves were scant, but within the Texas Dogman Triangle we can now identify no less than four, with John's being the most recent.

John takes his responsibilities as a landowner and cattle rancher seriously. He pays close attention to the movement of the indigenous wildlife, and he is accustomed to the seasonal patterns of their behavior. In November of 2021, he noticed a drastic reduction in the number of deer coming to feed on his land.

"Last year around deer season it was really weird, because we usually have a healthy crop of deer and there just wasn't any. Not anywhere near what it used to be like. And it threw me off, because we don't have hunters on the 1,800 acres that surround us, because it had sold, so they lost their hunting license. I'm the only feeder for a couple miles around, so you'd think they would be coming in. Same with the pigs. We used to have sounders of 30-40 and now you might see five or six at a time. That's it."

Many landowners find themselves faced with the opposite problem - an overabundance of deer and wild pigs. John relays his experience with reluctant honesty. His tone does not suggest hyperbole or embellishment. He speaks like a man who is resolute, yet perplexed, and unwilling to deny the reality that he is faced with. Above all, he sounds tired.

"I was down there in the stand one evening and I heard something big going through the brush. And I was thinking, okay, might have a big deer coming in, or there's a cow or something walking up. Then all of a sudden it sounds like something got into a den of coyotes, and there's I don't know how many coyotes going off like they were getting slaughtered, or attacked, or something like that."

Anyone who has heard an animal in distress can imagine the effect this would have on the unexpecting listener. The primal cries of mammals in pain activate, in most people, an urgent sense of both compassion and horror, and as mentioned earlier, can seem truly demonic or otherworldly.

"One, it sounded like it was being dragged away."

John clears his throat before continuing. After conducting dozens of interviews with researchers, witnesses, and other writers, one begins to get a sense for when someone truly believes what they are saying. I have been fortunate enough not to make the acquaintance of anyone who struck me as a snake oil salesman, but John's conviction is almost chilling.

"A couple nights later I had the dogs outside, and they started acting weird at the door wanting back in, so we let them in. And they're still acting weird. I'm like, *Okay*.

"I was about to go to work, so I grabbed my pistol and I go outside with a flashlight, start looking around and I see some eyeshine downhill.

"So, I think it might be a coyote or a mountain lion, or something like that.

"*Alright.*

"Eyes are a little bigger than normal.

"*Let's go check this out.*

"I walk down there, and it never walks away. Never looks away from me. Nothing. It sat there watching me as I'm walking towards it.

"I get about thirty yards from it, and I see that it is the biggest dog I have ever seen. I'm like, *okay, what the hell is this thing?*"

John responds to the presence of this potential threat with pragmatic resolve. If he is afraid, he pays the feeling no mind, but fear does not seem to be a part of the equation.

"Anything that can go after my livestock, I kill. So, I shot it. I shot it broadside - you could see the impact. You could see the flex of it whenever it hit. It turns and faces me, completely straight, and stands up."

I asked John to clarify - what did he mean by "stands up"? We've all seen a dog rise from a crouch to standing, and this is the image that my mind instinctively conjures.

"It stands up on its hind legs.

"And it's about six, maybe six and a half foot tall. A little taller than I am. I would estimate a bit heavier as well. I take a step towards it, and I put three more shots into it. Two to the chest, one to the head, just how I'm trained to do. The ones on the chest didn't really affect it much. The one to the head it kind of shook it off, glared at me, and then took off. I got the sense that I didn't hurt it terribly bad, but I got that I was going to be more problematic than it thought I was worth."

John is an experienced and proven marksman. He has served in the military and worked as a private security guard. As a hobby, he has won multiple shooting competitions in a variety of categories. He can make his way around a firearm with ease and knows beyond all doubt that the rounds he fired connected with his target.

"There was blood splatter on the ground. Just not that much. Not anywhere near where it should have been."

Then the creature walked away, seemingly unperturbed.[14] This was not the only time John would engage one of these bizarre, unnatural animals in close quarters.

"It seems like their bone density is a little too tight for most of your regular rounds and calibers, at least for chest and head. The younger male I did find out that

---

[14] Those familiar with the story of Skinwalker Ranch may find a striking parallel here. We will not explore Skinwalker Ranch in this volume as we lack the space to do so properly. One of the better-known aspects of that case, however, is that of an aggressive, oversized wolf which absorbed multiple gunshots before retreating into the woods, injured but alive.

softer tissue does work. It's still alive, but it at least got it to stop on the charge."

He then says:

"It did charge me one night, and that's when I figured out that it was a male. It had everything right there, and that's where I shot. I shot it right in the nuts with the first round. That put it down on the ground. While it was rolling around, I put three more into its abdomen and one into its neck. It took off on all fours away from me, and I put two more shots down at it coming from the back side. And this was with a five-five-six."

The 5.56x44mm is the standard ammunition used by NATO militaries. It has an average kinetic energy of 1,311ft. lb. - while my knowledge of firearms is limited, I was able to learn that the round is lethal at 200 yards, well beyond John's proximity to the animal in this encounter.

"I've seen coyotes that were the same way. If you don't get a perfect headshot or a heart shot, they'll keep going. They'll run two or three hundred yards before they realize they're dead."

John makes several allusions to the creature in the plural. I ask how many of the things he has seen on his property.

"I've got a breeding pair that stays on one side of the property, and they've got pups. And then another one that's a male, a smaller male that stays on the other side of the property, or in the middle. Either way, it avoids them (the breeding pair)"

I ask, "So at least four?"

"Oh yeah. More than four."

He describes the smaller male as a juvenile.

"The breeding pair were the first ones I encountered, and they keep their distance from me now. I didn't know what the hell I was dealing with, so I started researching."

John's research brought him to accounts of Dogmen and Sasquatch, and before long he got in touch with the North American Dogman Project. John has continued to document the strange activity on his property and reports that it is ongoing.

John shared several files with me. There are images of footprints, claw marks on trees, eyeshine high off the ground. One image shows something which blends with the background, standing near a fence, and John had highlighted the figure with a red circle to point it out. The deluge of files is almost overwhelming, and I have lost track of how much time I've spent poring over it.

Claw marks found on a tree (most likely oak) with John's hand shown for comparison.

Pictures of footprints measuring approximately 6 x 7 inches captured on John's property. One is shown next to a handgun for comparison. For reference, full grown mountain lions have an average track size of 4" with a general maximum of 5" in width. Coyote tracks average 2.5" in length.

Photos courtesy of John care of the author

"After that I was hunting in a pop-up blind in one of my fields, away from that feeder on the other side of my property. My wife says something big is coming down there and she thought it might have been a deer, but she couldn't get a good glimpse of it. She saw it as she was driving in, moving through the trees. So, I'm waiting, watching the direction it should be coming from, and that's when it comes out of the tree line. And this time I actually recorded it."

One of the attachments John sent is a video file, which shows a field at the edge of a wood line at dusk. There is a bluish hue to the scene, and the darker details of the ground blend with the shadows of the trees where they meet. In the center frame something is moving - an animal, dark in color, black, brown, or perhaps dark gray. It is difficult to make out the shape of the thing in the waning light, but the form of an animal walking across the field is immediately perceptible. The shape is roughly canine, though the video is blurry, shot from a great distance.

John explains:

"The video was taken with an iPhone at two hundred plus yards."

Sadly, the limitations of the device's digital zoom obscure the finer details, but there is something odd - perhaps something wrong - with the animal's movements.

"You can see it does not move right. It doesn't move like a coyote or a cat."

I cannot help but be reminded of the previously mentioned Kerrville Encounter, which took place in the year 2000. The animal in the video has a loping, up-and-down rhythm to its gait. The potential crossed my mind of an injured animal struggling to walk, such is the awkwardness of the movements, but the final seconds of the clip seem to contradict this assessment.

"Then towards the end of it, it stops, turns to me, and stands up."

I have watched the thirty second video enough times to lose count. I have slowed it down, run it in reverse, overlain filters to brighten the image, zoomed in, zoomed out, and applied every other rudimentary editing technique that my meager skill set includes to bring the action into better focus. My efforts were not fruitless but bore a small harvest. Brightening the clip brought out a few more meager details, making the shape of the animal easier to see against the dark backdrop.

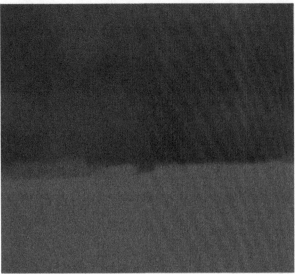

The figure walking in a "quadrupedal" stance

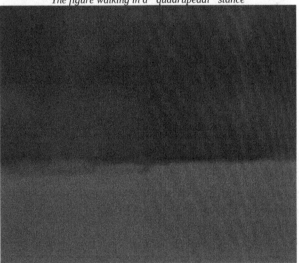

The figure after rising to a "bipedal" stance.

The details are obscured even after brightening. Nevertheless, what John describes does indeed appear to be what is taking place. Something moving out of the trees, into a field, and then rising to, what would appear to be, an upright position. While visibly on all fours, the animal's profile reminds one of a dog, wolf, moose, skinny bear, or perhaps something else entirely. The figure's silhouette becomes more difficult to make out after standing.

I am an expert in neither wildlife nor cinematography. I understand my hours of watching paranormal videos and documentaries have not qualified me to speak with total authority to the validity of any piece of evidence, never mind one this difficult to analyze. What can be written here with total confidence is that the video exists, is more than a bit odd, and has been rewatched by the writer an unreasonable number of times. It may also be argued that the animal is sitting down onto its haunches and not raising up on two legs, but its height never seems to decrease.

Additional photo captured by John using stationary cameras, circled portion provided by the witness.

I asked John point blank - "What do you think you're dealing with here?"

There is a long pause, heavy silence. You can tell this is a question he's asked himself before. He sighs before saying:

"Honestly, I don't know. It's just another type of animal. As far as I can tell it bleeds, it's just harder to kill. It's intelligent. It'll set traps. It'll do ambushes. It will test you. It will try to find your weakness, and it will try to exploit it."

I wondered if these experiences would force John to alter his routine, but little has changed about the way in which he manages his property. Previously he would venture out with a pistol, but now makes it a point to keep a rifle close at hand.

"I don't go out much at night anyway because there's no reason to."

If John's story is a hoax, it is an elaborate and long running one. The wealth of pictures and video he has provided indicates the presence of *something* on his land. I asked John to keep me apprised of future activity, and he graciously agreed.

As of July of 2022, his encounters with the creatures are ongoing. The breeding pair have gone mostly silent, perhaps retreating into the 1,800 acres of Hill Country beyond John's land. The aggressive juvenile male remains in proximity but has made fewer appearances in recent weeks.

As an isolated incident, John's case is compelling. But an additional encounter in the same area documented by the revered author and researcher Linda S. Godfrey certainly added more weight to the idea of a wolf-like offshoot in the Dallas/Fort Worth area, and oddly fit the profile of John's encounters almost to a T.

9
The Wolf on the Bridge - Sanger, Texas - 1985

In 1985 a witness identified as "Chuck" reported an encounter with an upright canine crossing a bridge near the town of Sanger. Chuck was not the original eyewitness, but states that the sighting was relayed to him by his brother. The beast was approximately five-feet-tall and stood in full view in the center of the bridge, illuminated by the headlights of a pickup truck. The creature lingered for a moment before walking away into the brush on two legs, and apparently the witness got a "good look" at it. Unfortunately, additional details regarding this case are not available. Searching "Sanger Werewolf Texas" produces results for an actor by the last name of Sanger who once played a character in a werewolf costume in a popular sitcom, but there is little else to be found online.

Fortunately, the venerated researcher and author Linda S. Godfrey documented this encounter in her 2012 book *Real Wolfmen: Encounters in Modern America.* Godfrey is generally considered the authority on this area of study in the modern era and is widely credited with drawing attention to the phenomena as a valid area of cryptozoological inquiry. The well-known Beast of Bray Road was first documented by Godfrey in a series of newspapers, and later in her eponymous book which would change the world's perception of what the term "werewolf" could mean.[15]

---

[15] At time of writing a mutual connection was working to put me in touch with the great Linda Godfrey. Sadly, Linda passed away in late 2022. Suffice to say that this work would not exist without her contributions to the field, and she has my utmost gratitude and respect.

When asked if I consider myself a paranormal "investigator" my immediate answer is a resounding "No." To compare myself in this regard to the likes of Jessi and Joe Doyle, known online as the investigative team Hellbent Holler, would be a bold and disrespectful leap. Jessi and Joe have been in the field (and the woods, and the swamps, and the mountains) investigating cryptozoological phenomena for over a decade. As mentioned previously, the duo has spent time in the Land Between the Lakes (LBL) documenting and researching phenomena related to the Dogman question for their series *The Werewolf Experiments*. I asked for their thoughts on a number of the aspects of this book, and they graciously agreed to contribute. When I asked general questions related to the Dogman phenomena, they made specific reference to the Sanger encounter – with no prior knowledge that it had made its way into the manuscript only days before.

From Jessi and Joe,

"The account is brief, mentioning a man named Chuck who wrote to Linda about a sighting near an old iron bridge west of Sanger, Texas. Chuck's brother was driving past the bridge in his pickup around 1:00 AM when he spotted an upright canine with light brown fur, it stood about 5-feet-tall and had yellow-green reflecting eyes. And that's the extent of the information given, so I dug a little deeper into this tale. Other than the commonly described attributes of the Dogman, the only other standout information is the presence of the creature at an old iron bridge. In addition to UAPs and a number of other phenomena, it seems as if these upright canids tend to appear in or around transitional spaces such as cemeteries, bridges, churches, boundaries, sacred places, and Indian mounds. Could it be that these entities are not natural animals, but creatures from another realm attracted to the energies of these places or can they journey into our realm at these 'crossroads'? Another interesting thing that threw up a flag at me about this case was its location. Sanger is in Denton County, Texas. Denton County is known for its number of historical iron bridges. There was even an initiative to preserve many of the bridges by the local historical society. One of these famed bridges, just south of the bridge I have determined to be the best possible candidate for this tale, is the Old Alton Bridge, or better known in paranormal enthusiast circles as Goatman's Bridge. A bridge haunted by the manbeast spectre of a man allegedly lynched by the KKK in the 1930's over the iron rails of that very throughfare. Could there be a connection between these supernatural bridge sightings and experiences in such close proximity?"

Jessi and Joe are right. The Alton Bridge is very close to Sanger - roughly twenty miles separate the two structures depending on the route. The story of the Goatman is a bit more notorious in paranormal circles than the Sanger Werewolf, and it straddles the line between folklore and urban legend. It also toes into the cryptozoology niche, as is the case with most of these stories. Defining the lines between cryptozoology, paranormal, supernatural, and so on is a common discussion, and legends such as these seem to blur the lines.

I did some digging into potential candidates for the bridge in question and identified an alternative – The Sam Bass Road Bridge at Clear Creek. The Sam Bass Road Bridge was originally constructed in 1908 and has since been swapped out for a modern replacement. The original truss frame of the bridge is placed parallel to the new and would seem to sit largely abandoned. It may be impossible to say in 2022, but Sam Bass does sit west of Sanger (and north of the Goatman's Bridge) as described in Godfrey's book *Real Wolfmen*. The iron bridge was also replaced with the present concrete structure in 2007, meaning that the antique byway was present at the time of Chuck's reported encounter. Whether or not this bridge is the one in question, Jessi and Joe relating this story to that of the Alton Goatman is an interesting connection.[16]

With two (so far) reports in the Dallas/Fort Worth area already examined, we now move on to a third. This case "bears" a striking and somewhat disturbing connection to the Beast of Bear Creek, particularly the stone carving which has characterized that story. This account, however, occurs a hundred or more years later, and unlike the Bear Creek Monster, we have an actual witness to account for this event.

---

[16] The question of paranormal phenomena related to old iron bridges is a deep rabbit hole. Other legends, such as the Donkey Lady in San Antonio on Old Applewhite, or the Pope Lick Monster of Louisville Kentucky (another goat-like entity) are closely associated with iron bridges. Yet another topic warranting considerable research for which we are ill equipped within this volume to properly explore.

10

A Werewolf in Paradise - Paradise, TX - 1996

The Paradise incident is one of the more exotic, perhaps "impossible" reports in the Triangle. It toes the line into the occult and supernatural, challenging the researcher who would conclusively attempt to claim that these entities are purely biological in nature. What's more, it involves a disturbing and visceral aspect of these reports which we would do well to remember:

Sometimes these beings are known to kill.

While the Beast of Bear Creek is rumored to have slaughtered humans and animals alike, we are, as stated, without any conclusive names, dates, or documentation to back up those claims. Sometime before 2010, veteran researcher and author Nick Redfern would receive a startling report from a shaken witness, though perhaps "victim" is also an accurate descriptor. The report first appeared in *Monsters of Texas* by Nick Redfern and Ken Gerhard and has appeared online in the intervening time as recently as this year.

This story was related to Nick Redfern by a rancher who goes by the name of Walter. In 1996, Walter was starting his day beneath the sunrise of a cool September morning. The ranch would be situated to the northwest of the city of Fort Worth, which is only a stone's throw from the megapolis of Dallas.

Walter happened upon a gruesome scene that morning. Surveying his fields, as he did every day, he caught sight of a disheveled heap amidst the grassy plain. Weather records reveal that there was both persistent rain and fog that September in the Dallas/Fort Worth area, and one can imagine the rancher approaching a blurry shadow on the misty plain, barely visible in the new morning light.

One of Walter's cows lay before him, dead not more than a few hours, perhaps already starting to smell. Disemboweled. Dismembered. Eviscerated. Aghast and appalled at such a sight, he alerted the authorities. The police paid a visit to Walter's land and took a report but did little else. The constabulary wrote the incident off to the activity of a natural predator, perhaps a mountain lion or wayward bear.[17]

Walter may have alerted animal control or Texas Parks and Wildlife but ultimately decided that he alone was the one best fit to protect his cattle. He armed himself and took to the outdoors, posting guard over his land through the wee hours of the morning. A few nights later, Walter caught sight of something through the scope of his rifle. He observed a shape moving through the field. It was muscular, hairy, with a profile and visage "like a large German Shepherd dog or a wild wolf."

It was alarming but not too out of the ordinary. There are plenty of wild dogs on the Texan plain, after all. Some of them are quite large. What disturbed Walter about this specimen, though, was its upright posture, free swinging forelimbs, and confident, stalking gait. There were only two legs beneath its hairy frame.

Walter didn't squeeze the trigger. He had the monster in his sights, the rifle was loaded, and he was surely confident in his ability to wield it. Yet, he only gazed on in abject horror and sick wonderment. His mind struggled to comprehend the madness unfolding in the

---

[17] Bears are rare in Texas, but there are confirmed sightings in the north and even known populations in the Southwest.

field. During this moment of hesitation, the beast entered the tree line and disappeared into the shadows.

Were this the end, it would be a chilling story. But Walter would make another discovery a short time later which would elevate this experience from disturbing to utterly bizarre and perhaps even Lovecraftian.

Walter later investigated the area where he had seen the man-wolf monstrosity. In the grass, he found something that he, at first, likened to an ordinary stone, but upon inspection, would certainly drain the color from his face.

The stone Walter found on his land after seeing the Man Wolf. Photo by Nick Redfern (used with permission)

It was a stone carving, depicting a face with fangs, narrow eyes, and slanted nostrils. It's an odd, nondescript item, and could easily be the work of some enterprising boy scout or even Walter himself.

But the resemblance to another stone carving - The Cleo Face, which we examined in a previous chapter - is striking.

Let us be as skeptical as we dare and assume that Walter invented the story and created the carving himself. Perhaps he had heard of Mr. Redfern through any of the numerous projects in which Nick has been involved (dozens of TV appearances, 41 books as of 2022, countless online articles, speaking engagements, writing credits, podcast interviews, etc.) and sent an inquiry with the idea in mind to pull a prank, perhaps score a few minutes in the limelight. People have told far stranger lies and gotten away with it.

Fine.

But there are two problems with the assumption that this was a hoax.

First, the almost uncanny resemblance of the Cleo Face to the Paradise stone (Paradise Face?) is impossible to overlook. They share prominent frontal canine teeth, a broad nose, and what appears to be narrow or slitted eyes. The Paradise Face also appears to be carved of limestone (I am not trained in geology and do not aspire to such, but my research seems to suggest this), and as stated by Michael Mayes, the Cleo Face was very likely carved into a limestone bluff.

Perhaps Walter was aware of the Cleo Face and the story of the Bear Creek Monster. It's possible. The legend has been part of the Hill Country for a long time. But as we have already learned, people who remember the Bear Creek story are few and far between. Cleo is defunct as an incorporated community and was so long before 2010. The newspaper article featuring the picture of the Cleo Face may have crossed Walter's radar and served as inspiration, but it was published in 1969 by the San Angelo Times and then republished by the Texas Folklore Society in 1999.[18]

This introduces only a very, very low probability that a rancher in rural Paradise would have seen the article in either incarnation. Next, even Michael Mayes' article on the *Texas Cryptid Hunter* website concerning the Beast of Bear Creek would not debut until 2012, meaning that online mention of the Bear Creek Monster would be scant to non-existent when Mr. Redfern received this report (other than, perhaps, another hypothetical website hosting the San Angelo Times article by Mike Cox).

The point here is that the chances of Walter already being aware of the Bear Creek Monster are perhaps fifty-fifty. However, the likelihood of him having seen a picture of the Cleo Face such that he could recall it and imitate it with his own version years later are, putting it one way, not so evenly balanced. He either saw it in 1969 and remembered it for about forty years and then reported it to Mr. Redfern, or he ran across it randomly after 1999 in a very obscure, esoteric publication put out by the Texas Folklore Society and thought to himself:

Yes! This is what I will make a hoax about!

The problem with this scenario, of course, is that Mike Cox's article on N.Q. Patterson does not mention werewolves, dogmen, or monsters. Walter could not have learned about a potential Dogman connection to the Cleo Face from the article even if he'd read it. This argument is in some ways a "dog chasing its own tail" and entirely dependent upon whether Walter was or was not aware of the Cleo Face, but there is more to it.

---

[18] San Angelo is four hours away from Paradise by car and the San Angelo Times is a local newspaper; it is not likely that it was available in DFW in 1969.

The second argument against this incident being a hoax may be a bit more concrete, though admittedly it only proves correlation.

There are three other significant Dogman encounters in the Dallas/Fort Worth area, which are detailed in this book (see the Maps section). Were Walter trying to jump on some sort of "spooky bandwagon" he would be picking an odd hill on which to plant his flag. As we have noted, the Dogman phenomena was not as hot in 2010 as it is today. Some of Linda Godfrey's books were in circulation, but the documentaries and community content which have recently brought so much celebrity to the beast were not. This is also assuming that Walter reported the sighting in the year of publication.

We have also discussed the Sanger encounter, which took place in 1985, but was not reported until 2012 in Linda Godfrey's *Real Wolfmen: True Encounters in North America.* Sanger is only about forty miles from Paradise, making the location almost uncanny. It seems very unlikely that Walter was given an advance copy of Ms. Godfrey's book two years shy of publication.

Another report which comes up later is The Collin County story, which the NADP website lists as occurring in 2018, and it was submitted to their database in April of that year. It was certainly not publicly available in 2010.

John's encounters (which are ongoing as of 2022) take place very close to Dallas/Fort Worth as well, and while he has asked that the name of his city of residence be kept confidential, they are still a part of the Dallas/Fort Worth cluster of sightings. These sightings were not reported until 2022.

What we are left with are two stone carvings with very similar faces, tied to two men who never met, separated by a century. They are both made of limestone, and they are both inexplicably linked with Dogmen, Werewolves, Man Wolves, etc - even if only in the minds of the lovers of folklore.[19] The revelation of a possible connection between these two cases sent chills down my spine, as have many of my forays into the Texas Dogman Triangle.

I had the opportunity to meet Mr. Redfern in October of 2022 during production of *The Dogman Triangle: Werewolves in The Lonestar State* and asked about this potential connection. He heard me out and entertained my theory but stated that he did not feel the Beast of Bear Creek has any link to the Cleo Face. Indeed, the connection is tenuous at best, but Mr. Redfern kindly consented to the inclusion of the photo of the "Paradise Face" in this book (he also autographed my copy of *Monsters of Texas,* crossing a long-time goal off my bucket list). The reader is invited to draw their own conclusions here, as in all other areas we will examine.

There is another story, somewhat in this genre concerning stone carvings and werewolves, but it is far - far - removed from the Triangle. This chilling tale is known as the saga of the Hexham Heads.

The story takes place in 1971 England. Two young boys were digging in the family garden when they happened upon a pair of stone carvings resembling human heads. They were roughly the size of a child's fist. The timeline is long and fantastic, but in short, the heads brought a guest along with them - a werewolf. The creature

---

[19] Walter would tell Nick that he believed that cultists were the root cause of his problems and were responsible for creating the carving and the appearance of the limestone face. If the story of Bear Creek is to be believed, the Cleo Face depicted a practitioner of dark and forbidden magic who could transform into a similar upright hound.

terrorized the family's neighbors before the heads were given away to an archaeologist. The werewolf returned, this time haunting the new owner. The artifacts are said to have been passed from person to person until they became lost to history, and they are currently unaccounted for.

11
The Converse Wolfman - Converse, Texas - 1850-1960

Converse, Texas is a city which runs almost imperceptibly into the north of San Antonio. Converse natives will tell you that they most certainly do not live in San Antonio *thank you very much*, and San Antonio residents will likely agree, though both cities share the 210-area code for local phone numbers. Converse was chartered in 1881 and named for the chief engineer of the Pacific railroad at the time, Major Converse. Today, the city boasts a population of over 11,000. In the early 1900s, however, the population of Converse was less than 100, just under 200 even after World War II. A significant boom for a town of only about six square miles.

Almost Lost to Time

This encounter is set at the close of the 1800s, when neighbors lived miles apart and news traveled slowly. This tale, which took place at the turn of the century, will serve to take us down a path that we have yet to travel in this book. It bears a darker, more grisly tone than many of the incidents we have examined thus far. It is also the only known human fatality resulting from an encounter with a strange, wolf-like creature within the Texas Dogman Triangle.

The tale tells of a farmer, as many residents of Converse were in those days. The man, who is not named and so will simply be called "the farmer" had a son, approximately age 15 when the story begins. The farmer sent his son off on a task one day. The young man's duty was to shoot and bring home a deer. Some interpretations of the story purport that the young man was not quite the hardened outdoorsman that his father wished for him to be, and that the hunt was meant to serve as a rite of passage.

This would not have been out of character for a family in rural Texas in the early part of the 20th century. Hunting was one of few accessible ways to obtain meat, and other protein sources were scarce. The young man proceeded to the woods into an area known locally as Skull's Crossing, relying on his lifetime spent in the untamed Texas countryside.[20]

The reader should note that the Texas scrublands are not a thing to trifle with, even if one is accustomed to them. Snakes, scorpions, wild cats, and plenty of other dangerous fauna are in abundance. Steep drop-offs, jagged rocks, and dry creek beds make up a minefield of opportunities to trip, twist an ankle, or break a leg. This is saying nothing of the elements. Summertime temperatures can easily exceed one hundred degrees Fahrenheit, and in an age without air conditioning, people were subjected to the heat without reprieve.

The farmer's boy traveled an unknown distance into this rugged wilderness, as the location of his home is also not specified anywhere. It must have been slow going as the boy made his way through the forest. Eventually, the young man came across what he likely at first thought to be a wolf or coyote.[21] Unfortunately, instead of any familiar canine-like creature, the young man encountered something far more terrifying: a monstrosity standing on two legs, with prominently pointed ears, sharp teeth, and a muscular build. Perhaps it snarled at him. Perhaps he screamed as he ran away. We can only imagine any number of details lost

---

[20] Whether this was to be his first solo hunting trip is unclear, but he must certainly have been on previous hunts with his father. Hunting was, and still is, an activity interwoven with daily life for many Texans.
[21] It is important to recall that wolves were still present in the wilds of Texas at this time and would have been commonly encountered.

to time, but what we do know for certain is that the creature pursued the boy.

He made a frantic return to the ranch, most certainly out of breath and red from exertion. He had returned home with his firearm but without the kill his father had expected. Words such as *beast, monster, demon,* or *werewolf* may have been used. But the farmer, a man set in tradition and uninterested in *monsters,* did not hesitate to order his son to return to the woods. He was not permitted to come home without completing his task. Perhaps an argument ensued. Perhaps the boy pleaded. Perhaps he fell back on tradition and duty and steeled himself against the horrors of the wilds he had so recently glimpsed. We will never know for certain. Regardless, he did as his father bade him and set off once more on the hunt.

A considerable amount of time passed. The boy did not return. Concerned, the farmer gathered what help he could and set off into the woods in search of his son. The earlier discussion of monsters surely nagged at the back of his mind. It is not known how long the search lasted, but it could not have taken more than a few hours for the farmer to locate his son - and the unnatural abomination the farmer had refused to believe in only a short time earlier.

The boy was dead. Hunched over his mangled and bloody corpse was a horrid monstrosity (*beast, monster, demon, werewolf*) bearing traits both canine and humanoid. It was muscular with long arms and sharp claws. A maw of savage teeth. Thick fur, dark gray or brownish black. Seven-, eight-, perhaps nine-feet-tall. By now, this description should be one that is familiar - an archetypal cynocephalus. The assembled party opened fire on the creature, but it fled into the woods and was never - as far as we know - seen again.

The farmer was left to mourn his son and forever regret not believing the young man's story. One can imagine the farmer spending long nights wallowing in regret, watching out the window, or perhaps stalking through the woods with a rifle in hand, eager for a chance at revenge. The story purports that either he did not live long after that incident or became a recluse. Regardless of the man's fate, this is where the story of the Converse Werewolf ends.

One thing of note is that Converse was a German settlement, much like the Fredericksburg. It is not too difficult to imagine that the people who settled in the area would have brought with them stories of bipedal wolves from their homeland, or that these stories would hang around into the late 1800s or early 1900s. As mentioned previously, werewolf mythology was prevalent in Europe for hundreds of years, and Germany was no exception. The residents, only a few generations removed from the early settlers, would remember the traditional stories of the lycanthropic fiends of their ancestors. A horrendous story involving the death of a young man because of an animal attack may have morphed from a tragic retelling of an actual misfortune to a paranormal folk tale. Wolves, after all, did exist in Texas during this period, and one or more large specimens may have been the root of this bleak old saga.

But what of the witnesses? What about the hunting party who accompanied the farmer in search of his son? Who was this farmer, what was his name, and does his family still live in the area? Why would settlers, or the near descendants of settlers of the Hill Country mistake a regular wolf for a two-legged fiend? Did no one write this down when it happened? Emboldened by the spirit of the anonymous farmer's son, I went hunting.

Comments from Lyle Blackburn

Lyle Blackburn is a name that is likely familiar to denizens of the unsolved. The veteran writer and investigator is known for being the go-to guy when it comes to cases such as Momo, or The Missouri Monster, which rose to infamy in the 70s. He is also the modern chronicler of the story of Boggy Creek, a rash of well documented sightings of a Sasquatch-like cryptid that occurred in Fouke, AR around the same time as the Momo case. Modern films such as the documentaries *Momo: The Missouri Monster* and *The Beast of Boggy Creek* by Small Town Monsters have brought the case into the spotlight for a new generation. Lyle was significantly involved in both productions. His books on both cases are impactful, if not also essential, entries to any researcher's paranormal library.

As he has explained, the Dogman phenomena has inevitably crossed his radar. In the summer of 2022 Lyle produced an episode of his podcast *Monstro Bizzarro* titled "Southern Werewolves." The timing couldn't have been better – Mr. Blackburn agreed to be interviewed for the writing of this book days before the episode was slated for release, unbeknownst to me at the time. The fact that one of my most admired authors and I were researching this same case around the same time was enough of a synchronicity to provide affirmation that I was on the right track.

In his podcast episode he details an encounter he experienced as a teenager which does fall in line with what some might suspect as being Dogman activity. Specifically, he heard vocalizations in a graveyard of all places. Since the witness in question (an experienced cryptozoologist) is hesitant to label the creature thusly, we will not do so either. I did however ask Lyle about the origins of the Converse Werewolf, and it seemed his research had led him down avenues like my own.

"There's no newspaper article or anything on that one," Lyle explained when I inquired about a source for the story.

"I don't think it's something that somebody made up because it's been out there for a while, but to me it's definitely more a quote-unquote urban legend that just sort of gets thrown into the Dogman-werewolf thing. Although some have speculated that it could have been a Sasquatch. It just depends how they want to spin it really."

Parallels with Modern Cases

This story bears commonalities with other, more modern, lycan-based encounters. We have already mentioned The Land Between the Lakes, a sprawling national recreational area which is housed by both Tennessee and Kentucky. It is notorious for an alleged Dogman attack in the 1980s in which multiple people were said to have been killed. Additional testimony by modern witnesses indicates that violent attacks by Dogman in this area are still ongoing or have at least occurred recently. This is discussed at length in *American Werewolves,* the 2022 documentary film by Small Town Monsters. The Converse incident seems to fit the profile of violence associated with these other reported fatalities. Mangled corpses being fed upon by an impossible nightmare, leaving permanent mental scars on those who are left behind to recount the story. Given the age of this legend, it seems reasonable that there is such a lack of evidence.

Some online sources state that the event may have occurred as recently as 1960, but this seems highly unlikely given that not even the name of the farmer can be conclusively determined. Such a grisly misfortune befalling a Converse local would surely have been covered by at least one local newspaper. Certainly, the story would have been picked up in nearby San Antonio. The late 1800s seems a more likely place in history for something like this to occur, but without any known documentation, this is only a somewhat-educated guess.

Moving to the north, we find another tale of a bloodthirsty wolf-adjacent creature. But this one is accompanied by dates, named witnesses, and specific locations unlike its cousin in Converse. Also, unlike the Converse Werewolf, this story was covered by more than one newspaper. Fortunately, this monstrous anomaly was only known to feed on livestock.

That is, of course, as far as we know.

12

The Beast of Plum Creek - Lockhart, Texas - 1980

Calf-killing monster stalks Plum Creek, ranchers assert

Between Austin and San Antonio, and very close to Converse, is the town of Lockhart. In 2020 the census listed a population of around 14,000, and the city is growing quickly due to the influx of people moving to Texas from out of state. About thirty miles from Austin and an hour away from San Antonio, Lockhart's location makes it a commutable distance from major population centers for those looking to save a few thousand dollars on housing. Like most of central Texas, the city is surrounded by hills and valleys, plains and woods, creeks and ranches, and so on. The Comal and Guadalupe Rivers, as well as Canyon Lake - three of the best known and most loved bodies of water in Texas - are within an hour's drive, give or take, along with countless other Hill Country attractions and destinations. As seems to be the pattern in central Texas, Lockhart has its share of haunted spots and urban legends. By now it might seem that every town in the state has at least a few resident ghosts, but Lockhart has something else entirely.

Specifically, it was once the home of a creature with a savage temperament, a voracious appetite, and a terrifying visage. Stories of cattle mutilation characterize its activities, in a time before "cattle mutilation" was a widely circulated term. This specific unfriendly beast is known to residents of Lockhart and those who tell the story as the Beast of Plum Creek.

Plum Creek is better known historically as the location of the Battle of Plum Creek. In 1840 white settlers clashed with the Native American Comanche people, with both sides inflicting heavy losses. Most search results for "Plum Creek Lockhart" or similar queries lead to articles concerning the sad legacy of this significant historical event.

Our interest in Lockhart and Plum Creek, however, begins 140 years later. On May 29th of 1980, The Austin American Statesman ran a sensational headline:

Calf-killing monster stalks Plum Creek, ranchers assert.

Texas became known for the death of livestock by strange creatures in the 2000s when the Texas Terror Dog first began making headlines. However, as Dr. Kristina Downs of the Texas Folklore Society states, people in Texas have been seeing strange canine creatures for a very long time. The Plum Creek Monster arrived on the scene almost thirty years before the Terror Dog's first media appearance, and it demonstrated a predilection towards preying on cattle.

One rancher, a man named Pete Shulz is quoted in the Statesman as having lost seven calves to the beast, the bodies of two never being found. The corpses which were found were badly mangled - specifically, disemboweled - and Shulz is purported to be but one of several ranchers who lost livestock during the series of attacks.

The description of the monster has become familiar at this point in our examination of Texas canines - an oversized dog with pointed ears, crouching upright in a posture both bizarre and frightening to observe. Rancher James Witter describes the animal as having the "pointed ears of a Doberman" as well as "a bobbed tail, long snout and pointed ears." Later in the article Witter attributes it as looking somewhat like a Hyena,

"But I am not saying that is what it is. I put it this way - it wasn't no wolf."

Until very recently, there was little more to be said for James Witter's testimony. He has spent close to the last fifty years in relative anonymity, but through a fantastic turn of luck I was able to meet him in October of 2022.

After reading an early draft of this volume, my friend Heather Moser took this lead and ran with it. Not three months later, I was standing on Mr. Witter's property near modern-day Lockhart, hearing the story of the Plum Creek Monster from one of only four of the original witnesses.

Mr. Witter adamantly asserts that he is not aware of the Plum Creek Monster committing any actual cattle murder, and that the appearance of the beast was not nearly as dramatic as the media would purport. His wife would corroborate this statement, and both expressed their frustration at the way in which the media had sensationalized the monster's appearance and activities. In truth, both were hesitant at first to speak with Shannon Legro, also present during our visit, and I, even though our arrival was scheduled, and our agenda had been explained in detail prior-to. They would go on to tell us that the true story of the Plum Creek Monster's initial appearance is not as salacious as the newspapers would have us believe.

Mr. Witter, along with three other witnesses, saw two large, unidentifiable animals that he described, even nearly fifty years later, as looking like a hyena. It was surreal to hear him tell the story in person, and hear him say out loud, "It wasn't no wolf."

James said that the men agreed to keep the story quiet for fear of ridicule. Why whip the locals into a frenzy without cause? Unfortunately, this agreement would not last long.

Two of the other witnesses, while making their regular visits to a local "beer joint" as Mr. Witter described it, 'unleashed' the story and began rolling the snowball which would soon become an avalanche. James did not give the names of these men, but states unequivocally that he adhered to the original agreement and kept the story to himself. When we assured Mr. and Mrs. Witter that our intent was to tell the story of The Plum Creek Monster as they remembered it, without embellishment for dramatic effect, they warmed to us, and not only shared the details of the case, but also provided us with another destination.

Today, Plum Creek is crossed by Flores Drive, a two-lane country back road. Where the road meets the creek, a concrete bridge allows passage. Mr. Witter directed us not only to the infamous creek, but to the exact location of one of the monster's appearances. He stated that the location was technically private property. He assured us, though, that if we were approached, we need only say that we are friends of James Witter.

After some driving and a few wrong turns, we parked our cars on the side of Flores Drive and sauntered down the slope within sight of Plum Creek.

It is not difficult to imagine all sorts of exotic wildlife lurking in the thick vegetation, even though less than a mile west is a town of over ten thousand. A rock from the creek bed now sits on my bookshelf, and as Shannon, myself, and the Small Town Monsters film crew approached the creek a calm seemed to settle over the area. I will not say or assume that it was a supernatural event, but to visit this place after so long was a truly cathartic experience.

Plum Creek in 2022, picture by the author.

On our visit to Lockhart and Plum Creek there were no werewolves in sight. We also encountered no ghosts of the famed Battle of Plum Creek, though the area is undeniably beautiful. To my knowledge, there are no accounts of the creature being sighted since the initial reports, though only time may tell if the Beast will make any future appearances.

I consulted with another colleague and friend, Kenzie Gleason, a paranormal investigator and cryptozoologist on this case. She had this to say,

"I think the cross section between folklore and cryptozoology is incredibly important and needs to be more deeply explored. Folklore didn't come from nothing, and I've definitely been quoted a handful of times saying that I think there is a lot of truth to folklore, especially with the way it's progressed in the modern world."

Kenzie would provide this statement well before I met James Witter. It would seem she was correct.

There is one feature mentioned in the animal's description which stands out, beyond the fact that it appears to be some sort of inexplicable humanoid.

The animal is described as sitting upright "like a monkey." Ape-like features are often mentioned in correlation with encounters with upright canines, such that the debate over whether a given sighting should constitute a Dogman or Sasquatch report is ongoing. The reader may recall that Joedy Cook of the North American Dogman Project postulates that older encounters with ape-like beings would do well to be assessed with the possibility of the Dogman in mind, perhaps allowing us to differentiate between the two hypothetical species. Michael Mayes presents a contrasting viewpoint - he presents the opinion that most Dogman encounters are likely mis-identified Sasquatch but remains open to the possibility of a separate species of canine persuasion, as discussed earlier in this work.

To the point however, it is worth noting that San Antonio - a mere hour away by car - is home to the previously mentioned Southwest Research Institute, which as of 2023 maintains a primate research facility. The possibility of an escaped primate from this facility making its way to Lockhart and then ravaging the local livestock is remote, but it should not be altogether discounted. Other potential cryptid encounters have been attributed to this facility, founded by the late patron of cryptozoology Thomas Baker Slick, Jr. Much could be (and has been) written on the strange synchronicities and history of both Mr. Slick himself and the institute which he founded.

Perhaps, however, the Beast of Lockhart has appeared since its 1980 debut. While incidents of cattle mutilation in the area have petered out since the frenzy of the Plum Creek Monster's exploits, similar incidents continue across the country. Might the beast have moved on to far off pastures?

An obscure newspaper article would give some credence to this. Also brought to my attention by Heather Moser, witnesses made similar reports in the southern portion of Austin, Texas around the same time. The Plum Creek Monster was alleged by some to have made an appearance over 40 miles north, leaving in its wake the mutilated bodies of farm animals.

Nearly fifty years hence, questions remain. What exactly was the Plum Creek Monster? Did it travel to South Austin? Did it kill any cattle? If not, what led to the reports of slaughtered cattle in the Plum Creek area around the time the creature was sighted?

This would not be the last time that the term "hyena-like" would be used to describe a potential Dogman encounter. Sam Houston National Forest awaits, and we will enumerate its strangeness in short order.

13

Nightmares in Collin - Collin County - 2018

We have examined three encounters near the sprawling metropolis of Dallas and Fort Worth - John's ranch, Sanger, and Paradise. But there is one more incident, set on the calendar between those already explored, which continues the pattern of behavior by the strange animals with which we are becoming so familiar. This is another sighting recorded by the North American Dogman Project.

We're fortunate to have the date and time of this incident. It was April 4th of 2018 - a Wednesday - and Jeff was returning home from work at approximately 12:00 AM. Let me paint a picture for you:

Jeff is used to the sounds of the night around his property, usually noting a few coyotes or the barking of the neighbor's dogs, but tonight is different. Something has changed. An odd chord is struck in the symphony of the night, and from that moment forward, our witness will likely never be the same.

"It sounded like a deep howl, but instead of the usual dog sound it stayed as one tone, and it was octaves deeper."

A chilling thing to imagine. It brings to mind the booming, brassy siren-like sound effect made popular in movie soundtracks composed by Hans Zimmerman. But this was only the start of the night's festivities.

The sound begins to move from yard to yard, sending every dog in the area into a hysterical fit of barking. As the sound draws closer, Jeff's own dog takes notice, and races off towards the fence line, adhering to her protector's instincts.

Then she freezes.

"I got up and I told her, 'Hey, come back in girl, it's ok.' She turned to me, and she sat there utterly frozen in fear. It took a few minutes to break her out of this, and she bolted to the back door."

Despite the eerie sounds coming out of the darkness and his dog's bizarre behavior, Jeff makes the decision to investigate. He pokes his head out of the rear gate of his yard and catches sight of a pair of "these amber colored eyes" sitting around five feet from the ground, trained on him. Jeff bolts back to his house, retrieves a knife from inside, and then goes back to the fence. He approaches the place where he'd seen the glowing set of eyes with caution, all to the sound of howling in the blackness. He admits that at this point he did not see anything, but when he reaches the spot where the eyes had been, the night falls silent. The howling comes to an abrupt stop.

"You could have heard a pin drop."

He hesitates a moment, and is then overcome with the sense that someone, or something, is watching him, hidden somewhere in the opacity of the night. He re-enters his own yard, shuts the gate and decides to smoke a cigarette on the porch before going inside, perhaps wishing to see how the strange events would play out. It wasn't long before the howling resumed, but this was just a prelude of things to come.

Now, the sounds are coming from the neighbor's backyard. These neighbors were in possession of two German Shepherds. This is a breed which has a reputation for being fiercely protective and physically powerful, plenty of their ancestral wolf DNA still engrained.

"I first heard this guttural growl noise unlike anything I've heard before, then one of the shepherds shrieked, and then I heard the other got slammed against the fence. One thing led to another, and I heard my neighbor fire off a round, and then I heard this thing trail off."

It seemed that the 'thing' Jeff saw earlier in the trees with the glowing amber eyes had come back to trespass on his neighbor's property, itching for a fight. How far Jeff was from the source of the sounds and how close his neighbor's yard was to his porch is not specified, but the entity apparently attacking the neighbor's dogs is a disturbing detail. Likewise, the report does not detail whether Jeff and his neighbor ever spoke on the incident.

Jeff's story could end here, but he had a second encounter only a few nights later. According to the report shared by the NADP, this next event took place on the 23rd of April, not even four weeks later.

The howling resumed, but this time the howls were accompanied by heavy footfalls. They originated not in the neighbor's yard, but in the woods behind Jeff's house, perhaps near where he'd sighted the amber eyes a few weeks before.

"I heard the thumping of its feet and branches were snapping."

Jeff responded with more caution this time, citing his instinct to find cover from danger. He turned off the porch light and allowed his eyes some time to adjust, keeping them trained on the tree line beyond his property. Enough daylight was present for him to maintain a decent view of the nearest clearing, roughly twelve feet wide. This clearing seemed to be the source of the unsettling howls, and this would be confirmed for Jeff mere moments later.

Something stood up in the clearing, rising above the low trees and brush.

"I first saw the ears tall and sharp like knives. I then saw its head, followed by its broad shoulders and long arms. It stood there watching me for what seemed like forever until it turned and ducked down a little and took massive strides on two legs to walk off."

Pointed ears, broad shoulders, pronounced forelimbs, bipedal locomotion. We (the paranormal community at large, and the readers of this book), are becoming steadily accustomed to this description. It is unlikely that a man like Jeff, more concerned about returning home safely from work at midnight, is spending his off hours reading accounts of Dogmen on the internet or in books.

Why bother when one has ready access to the things themselves?

"I learned there was an encounter in Firestone County not very far from me. I hope to get reasonable evidence soon."

Some light research reveals the absence of a "Firestone County" in Texas, but two hours south of Collin is the county of Freestone. Sure enough, there is an encounter listed for this area, also on the NADP website.

14

Freestone County - 2016

To this day, I'm terrified to go out at night or in the early morning hours.

Freestone County lies just under eighty miles south of Dallas, placing it fairly close to the other reports coming out of that part of the Texas Dogman Triangle. It is adjacent to Houston as well as the Sam Houston National Forest, which we will explore later. Admittedly, there does not seem to be a heavy concentration of paranormality in this area, though nearby Troy is another known ghost town. Nevertheless, permit your author to outline a scenario for you, dear reader.

It was the time of year for hunting coyotes, our witness frequently spent this season on their grandparents' land, engaging in that very activity. They were well equipped, well-seasoned, and a good shot. Used to firearms, used to Hill Country wildlife, used to the whole kit and caboodle of humanity vs. nature.

"I was out at my grandparent's house, hunting coyotes, as usual, this time of year. I was hiking through my next-door neighbor's land, to get to the wood-covered land in the back. While I was hiking, I got the feeling I was being followed by something to my right. I stopped and switched the red tint on my headlamp to my spotlight but didn't see anything. Then I switched back to my headlamp and pulled my rifle back up and continued my hike."

The small details of the witness's trek are important. As we will note in other cases, what may seem like insignificant bits of unrelated data add to the likelihood of a story being true. Someone with the intent to lie may dream up any number of aspects to any number of stories, but this specific mention of the hiker's equipment denotes, at the very least, an understanding of what a person hunting in the Hill Country might carry with them. A head lamp with a red tint option and the obligatory firearm.

"It was 6:15 AM and the sun was just coming up. I was sitting in a hide I'd made the day before. That's when I saw something behind a group of trees on my left. It was crouched. I raised my rifle, looked through my scope and froze when I saw the creature staring back at me. I panicked and fired a shot off. That's when it stood up and took off, deeper into the woods. I sat there probably another 25 mins before I decided it was safe to head in and did so. Later that day, I grabbed my grandfather and we both went out to where I had seen the creature when it stood up on 2 legs and took off. We measured where I had seen it and it was roughly 7 1/2 feet tall.

To this day, I'm terrified to go out at night or in the early morning hours."

Our disadvantage in this case is that the witness does not provide a proper description. We may insert the upright beast with pointed ears and yellow eyes through deduction, but the sequence of events could easily include a being more representative of a member of the ape family. In truth, it could be anything.

Nevertheless, what we see is another example of a competent outdoorsman struck with terror and disbelief at the sight of an unknown animal. Presumably, this witness would be able to make swift identification of a wolf, coyote, or mountain lion. Likewise, this would not be the type of witness to suffer lingering psychological or emotional aftereffects if the subject of their sighting were any known member of the local fauna.

15

The Lakeside Wolfman - Meridian, Texas – 1977

Laura ran. Her sneakered feet fell heavy on the dusty gravel path. The terrain was uneven, but she kept her footing. Trees flew by on either side, her vision a blurry wash of green and brown, her breath ragged in the Hill Country heat. But she kept running.

She was tempted to look back. To see if the thing was pursuing her, to see if she had any chance of escape or if she was moments from her demise.

Though it might be better not to know.

She didn't look. She didn't dare divert one fraction of her attention from her desperate flight towards safety for risk of slowing down, stumbling, falling. To do so would almost certainly mean death. The thing behind her could not have anything behind its snarl but malintent.

Survival depended upon flight.

In 1977, Laura was camping in Meridian State Park with her boyfriend, David. One evening, she took a stroll at dusk along one of the park's many wooded paths, this one wrapping around Meridian Lake in the center of the campground. In an area she describes as the "Bee Caves" Laura spotted the shadow of what she first thought to be a large man. She walked cautiously, quietly, careful not to hit her head on any low hanging branches or catch her foot on a jagged rock. After passing the shadow, she heard what she describes as a "huffing sound" coming from behind her. When she turned, she saw something far more frightening than a "large man." She screamed, "at the top of my voice."

And she ran.

Laura returned to the campsite in a state of panic, still screaming. When David asked after the source of her distress, she offered one word in explanation.

"Werewolf!"

One can imagine an incredulous stare and the assumption that she must be joking. But Laura was deadly serious and stuck to her story despite anyone's disbelief.

"Of course, no one believed me, and of course the giant wolf man was gone."

The next morning, Laura again walked the circumference of the lake, this time accompanied by her boyfriend. When they came to the location of her sighting (the Bee Caves) she states that her chest tightened, panic once more setting in. To her relief, the creature was nowhere in sight.

But it had not vanished without a trace. Imprinted in the mud, near the location of Laura's initial flight, was an animal track. An exceptionally large one which neither could identify. David knelt to examine it more closely.

"That's no dog print," he said, "nor is it a bear paw print. It's time to go home."

Laura left, and reports in 2019 that she never returned to Meridian State Park.

Meridian, Texas is in Bosque County, roughly fifty miles northwest of Waco. The state park which shares its name lies just to the southwest of the city along Highway 22. Today the park is home to just over five trekkable miles for the intrepid hiker, and the Bosque trail (so named for Bosque County) circles the lake. This may be the trail upon which Laura had her sighting. The "Bee Caves" to which Laura refers are likely an overlook of rocky ledges which provide a view of the central body of water.

There are cabins available for rent on the lake for $50 per night with limited amenities, including nearby showers, electricity, and climate control. An additional set of screened structures are also available for groups of up to eight campers. There is an array of semi-primitive to primitive outdoor sites on hand which can accommodate groups as large as 72.

All this is to say that the details regarding the location of Laura's story can generally be confirmed. Meridian State Park does have a large lake circled by a walking trail, numerous caves, and rentable cabins. It is heavily wooded, and the land surrounding the park is rural and undeveloped. There are scattered homesteads and ranches along the country back lanes, but the entire county of Bosque was home to just over 18,000 in 2020. In 1977, estimates state that Bosque had just over 12,000 residents.

The profile of this location is consistent with other areas of suspected Dogman activity. Ample brush cover. Acres of trees. A relatively small population spread out over a wide area where many neighbors live far apart. A state park with plenty of government-protected space. As observed elsewhere, there may be room for one or more large animals to move undetected between sources of water and food, exploiting these unobserved tracts of private and public land. Meridian lends itself to this possibility.

In 1977, one camper may have been lucky (or unlucky) enough to encounter one. Laura's sighting is not accompanied by photographic evidence, yet it strikes a strong chord in the symphony of Texas Dogman activity. Slotting neatly into the middle of the Triangle, it lies between and adjacent to the southern sightings that make up the Wolf Mountain Cluster and the harrowing encounters which began taking place to the north near Dallas/Fort Worth in 2021. 1977 places it very early in the timeline of modern anecdotal encounters, shortly before the Plum Creek Monster ravaged the livestock of Lockhart in 1980. It is also another story of a witness terrified by what they can only describe as a "wolf man," which by now has become a familiar succession of events. Laura's use of this term is significant.

A quick internet search reveals that more than thirty werewolf centric films were released in the seventies, many of them originating in Mexico, and some (more than one) featuring popular luchador wrestler and movie star Rodolfo Guzmán Huerta, better known by his stage name, El Santo.[22]

There may be other samples of media content which inspired Laura to shout *"Werewolf!"* Although, it is unlikely that she would have viewed or even been aware of them all. Would one, perhaps two have been enough to cement the concept of *werewolf* in her mind? Did she confuse a normal animal or a tall human being for a paranormal monstrosity? Or did Laura really see an upright canid, the likes with which we are becoming all too familiar?[23]

---

[22] Lovers of horror, science fiction, camp, pulp, parody, and the paranormal are encouraged to seek out El Santo's films. They are a delicacy to lovers of the bizarre.

[23] This story was shared with *True Horror Stories of Texas* in 2019. There do not seem to be any additional sightings connected to Meridian State Park - at least, none of which we are currently aware.

16

Sam Houston National Forest - 1977 & 2018

Sam Houston National Forest is one of four national forests in the state of Texas. This expansive state park consists of over one hundred and sixty-three *thousand* acres, by far the largest single plot of land we will investigate. Naturally, it is the home of the wildlife typical of the Texas Hill Country. Deer are the most popular game animal, followed by squirrels, but duck hunting and fishing are also a regular pursuit. It is a frequent destination for campers and hikers and is so vast that the three counties of Walker, San Jacinto, and Montgomery all fall within its borders.

There are various tales of upright wolves in the Sam Houston National Forest area, spaced a modest number of years apart and coming from a variety of sources.

One is from a thread posted on Reddit in 2021 by a user going by the handle tintin2605. It is short, the details are slim, and it seems to deal mostly with auditory phenomena. Tintin2605 describes a sound "like a mixing between the yelling of a woman and howling of a coyote, maybe just some night birds," which would fit the bill of other suspected "Dogman howls." One may think back to the previous encounter which took place in Pedernales Falls State Park, describing similar noises.

Tintin2605 turned out to be a man named Justin. Justin still lived in the Sam Houston area as of late 2022, and I was able to meet him and hear his story first hand. He repeated his story without deviation, describing an isolated area with specific rules regarding noise and rowdy behavior after dark. The bestial howl he heard that night left him with a lasting impression and meeting him in person verified his sincerity.

He also stated that "a couple" had a sighting of a Dogman-like creature within the national park "a couple years back." Supposedly, a husband and wife witnessed a doglike animal standing on two legs. Shortly before they saw the mysterious being, their dog had inexplicably disappeared. They attributed the disappearance to the strange upright animal. This idea of Dogmen or werewolves attacking other canines, specifically domestic dogs, is yet one more of the recurring elements in these harrowing tales.

A video posted on YouTube in 2022 would seem to provide a first-person account of the couple's story. The tale first appeared on *True Horror Stories of Texas*, submitted by a user named Ryan P.

Ryan recalls an incident in September of 2018 where "something" snatched his dog and dragged her off into the tree line. He didn't see the fiend in question - at least not right away - and apparently never saw his dog again. Ryan and his wife went looking for the dog in the area she had disappeared but found not a trace of their beloved pet.

"There were no signs of a struggle, no blood, no fur, nothing. Like whatever took my dog just vanished."

Not too long after that, Ryan was sitting on his porch at 4 AM enjoying a cigarette. Abruptly the forest fell deadly silent, bereft of any of the normal sounds which accompany that hour - yet another repeating aspect of these meetings with frightful creatures.

Ryan swept a spotlight across the tree line, and in its beam caught what he calls,

"The biggest wolf head I have ever seen."

Ryan made note of the thing's green eyes and pointed ears. The animal stared back at him, apparently unperturbed. The head sat four or so feet off the ground. A large specimen to be sure, but nothing too terribly out of the ordinary.

Until it placed a hand - Ryan specifically states that it was a hand, not a paw - on the side of a tree trunk and stood up. Onto two legs.

Ryan had seen enough but didn't dare take his eyes off the thing. He reached behind his back and fumbled for the doorknob, managed to turn it after a moment, and rushed back into the house.

His wife was asleep - after all, it was 4:00 AM - and he roused her frantically, insisting that she come to the front of the house and look outside to confirm what he'd seen. Perhaps alarmed by the hysteria in his voice, she rolled out of bed without protest and accompanied her husband to the living room.

Fortunately, or perhaps not fortunately at all, the awful thing was still in sight. Ryan notes that he knew his wife had seen it due to the shocked expression on her face. The animal dropped onto all fours and walked back into the trees. Ryan states in no uncertain terms that he remains "scarred" from the incident, afraid to go near the woods at night and is especially jumpy in response to unexpected noises.

"People need to know that these things are out there. I'm not saying people should go out there and obliterate them all if they could even find them, but people should be aware that they exist and they're out there. But believe me, I've tried telling others and they just laugh and make jokes and think I'm nuts which makes the people who have encounters shut down and not share their experience."

If these examples were the only talk of wolfish specters in Sam Houston, they would still be worth looking into, but there is more. Gary Wiggins, an archaeologist and Texas native, purports to have had an alarming encounter with one of these creatures inside Sam Houston National Forest in 1977. This interview was featured on the podcast *Dogman Encounters Radio*, in Episode 50 dated July 8th, 2015.[24] This aside, Mr. Wiggins' encounter would have taken place the very same year as Laura's sighting in Meridian State Park, an environment of far fewer acres but very similar topography.

Justin would not be the only witness I would meet in this area. During the filming of *The Dogman Triangle: Werewolves in The Lone Star State* I would encounter numerous others who described beings which perfectly fit the werewolf profile we have become so versed in. They name these beings "the monsters," and describe specimens ten to eleven feet in height with glowing red eyes. Their encounters also go back decades, and their families have told tales of these creatures for as long as any local can remember.

Perhaps a modern-day investigation into Sam Houston National Forest is warranted to shed additional light on what may be lurking between the trees, within the creeks and along the limestone ridges that define the near infinite acres--with, of course, great caution taken by the investigators.

---

[24] Attempts to reach Mr. Wiggins and the host of *Dogman Encounters Radio*, Vic Cundiff, have thus far proven unsuccessful.

17

The Werewolf of Vidor - Vidor, TX - 1978

One of the best documented cryptid reports in Texas, and perhaps anywhere else for that matter, is that of the Vidor Werewolf. This story has the benefit of being backed up by multiple witnesses, including law enforcement personnel. Dates and times are recorded in detail by an area newspaper, and there is no shortage of credible witnesses.

Vidor was chosen as a part of the far-east corner of the Texas Dogman Triangle for this very reason. Until recently, it was one of the few relevant stories to come out of the area. The seemingly continual modern run-ins with these creatures that are now being reported have provided a deluge of anecdotes, but the Vidor werewolf remains an incredibly detailed and chilling instance of an old-world monster clashing with modern-day humans.

Even in 2022 Vidor is a small town. In 1980 the population was just a little under 12,000 and had shrunk to around 9,700 as of 2020. A less than savory reputation for matters entirely unrelated to weird wolfy *googahs* will be near the top of most internet searches for "Vidor, Texas." One may even have to dig beyond the first page of Google to find details about this spooky story, but the information that is available is abundant.

Beckie Bussinger was eighteen years old. She had been married to her husband Bobby for only two weeks. They lived in a comfortable house which her father owned on a wooded lot, and Bobby worked for a tire company near Beaumont, a neighboring city where Beckie's parents also lived.[25]

A journalist reporting for the *Orange Leader* newspaper named John Rice wrote on June 20th of 1978:

"They knew when they moved into the area that previous tenants left because of strange occurrences during the night. An elusive figure roams the night, clawing at the window screens, howling, yelping like a wounded dog."

On Monday, June 19th at 11:30 PM Sheriff's Deputy Jack Reeves arrived at the Bussinger home. The young couple were in a state of near panic.

The chaos had begun earlier in the evening, right before or right after sundown. The moon "moved into full phase" and as darkness fell they heard something which chilled them to the bone. They described it as sounding like "a good sized dog fight."

Rice explains:

"The Bussingers told him that on Sunday night three of their dogs were believed killed. The hindquarters of two were maimed and the dogs have died. One is missing. All three are puppies of mixed breed, part of the eight dogs the young couple kept on the property."

---

[25] Today, the highways near Beaumont have a reputation amongst cross-country road trippers for always being under construction. In fact, most people traversing from Texas to Louisiana or vice versa will pass through a narrow, multi-mile stretch of concrete barricades and tire-killing ruts. Once, a construction worker using an industrial buzzsaw on a slab of asphalt sprayed hot molten gravel into oncoming traffic, a piece of which remained embedded in my windshield for years thereafter. But I digress....

As darkness fell, they heard more noises, these hitting much closer to their literal home. Scraping and tapping against the windows, something heavy repeatedly throwing itself against the exterior walls, and all of it against a backdrop of "an eerie barking" and "heavy footfalls." 261 miles south and almost forty years later - thirty-nine years, nine months and sixteen days to be precise - Jeff of Collin County Texas would give an almost identical description of the noises he heard during his own inexplicable run-in with an uncanny suspected wolf beast.

As the commotion continued, "a yelping filled the air," and Bobby decided that enough was enough. His home had been compromised. Beckie was in danger. He would not sit by and wait for the front door to fail or a window to shatter.

Bobby snatched his .12-gauge shotgun from the wall pegs on which it rested. He burst from the home as he readied his weapon. With a dire resolve he trained the barrel of the shotgun on a tall, upright, shaggy form at the edge of the tree line which bordered the backyard.

Six-feet-tall or more. The body was muscular, the hair thick, the eyes watchful.

"Werewolf."

Bobby's finger constricted around the arc of the .12 gauge's trigger. The beast lunged, jaws agape, hungry eyes locked on the young man, barely into his 20s, who had so readily thrown himself against the impossible.

There was a thunderous boom as the shotgun discharged. The round certainly hit the lycanthrope abomination dead-center. There was no way Bobby could have missed. Yet, it kept coming.

Bobby ran.

He barely slammed the door behind him before the creature fell upon him. After bolting it as securely as he was able, dialed 911. Deputy Reeves answered the dispatch, arriving shortly after the confrontation. Even not accounting for the shell-shocked young couple, the scene that awaited him was disturbing.

"He saw window screens torn 'by what appears to be bare hands.' Some of the frames are broken. Four screens were ripped off."

Many encounters with the bizarre and inexplicable end here, at this stage. Everything ceases after the initial run-in, after some sort of official or unified response. But the Werewolf of Vidor had yet to retire for the evening, and the Bussingers would not be the only witnesses that night.

Jack, Bobby, and Beckie discussed strategy. It was decided that Deputy Reeves would investigate the woods himself, alone, in search of the monster. He made a slow approach in the darkness, and heard "growling and howling, in the distance. It sounds like a cross between the sound a hyena makes and that of an injured dog. As I went into the woods, the sound came from further away and I knew it was backing off."

Beckie also told the Deputy that she used to pick berries along a well-defined path that leads into the woods - an activity she had since abandoned - and on one such afternoon stroll witnessed a lean-to structure made of branches far in the distance. She insisted that the creature made regular use of this path to enter and exit the woods beyond the property.

The good Deputy Jack Reeves returned to his vehicle. The plan was to drive away from the property, park under a streetlight a little further down the road and lie in wait for the monster to come back.

Less than five minutes after he re-entered the driver's seat his CB radio sang, crackling and squawking.

"It's back!"

Dispatch informed him that the prowler had returned once more scratching at the window screens and banging on the rear wall of the house. The eldritch fiend was nothing if not persistent.

Jack Reeves engaged the engine of the squad car, slammed on the accelerator, and pulled into the Bussingers' driveway "in seconds."

But the werewolf was already in retreat.

"It had backed off."

The Deputy turned on his squad car spotlight, swept the beam across the yard and finally caught sight of the thing. It stood at approximately fifty yards, between two trees which were set in a downward delta formation.

"It was between two small oaks that form a vee."

He continued, "I shined the spotlight and it moved into the woods."

The game of cat and mouse - or humans and wolf - needed to end. The Bussingers packed up their personal belongings while the heroic Deputy Reeves stood sentinel. They left the property that same night (or morning since Deputy Reeves arrived at 11:30 PM and had been pursuing the Bussinger's assailant for a considerable period) and went to stay with Beckie's parents in nearby Beaumont. At the end of the article, the sheriff's department promised to undergo a full investigation of the attack.

Beckie Bussinger told John Rice during her interview,

"I'm not going near that place until they find it. Whatever it is."

An upright, muscular, shaggy werewolf. Sketch by Mike Garcia.

There is a lot to unpack in this story. It checks off nearly every box on our list of convincing and credible evidence sought in cases dealing with the unsolved. Names, dates, locations, independent witnesses, a law enforcement response. Sadly, we are bereft of photographs.

Like the Converse Wolfman and the Dogmen of Dallas, the Werewolf of Vidor showed little to no aversion to being shot at point blank range. Those who encountered the creature were undeniably afraid (except, perhaps, Deputy Reeves). Like the Plum Creek incident only two years later, the animal is believed to have attacked and possibly fed upon domestic animals, in this case three of the Bussinger's eight dogs. It was also aggressive towards human beings, but retreated when Bobby called for reinforcements, much like Laura's encounter in Meridian State Park the year before. When Laura's boyfriend David accompanied her in search of the "wolf man" she had seen, it was nowhere in sight, but left evidence in the form of footprints.[26]

One of the small details shared in John Rice's piece is the address of the incident, where the Bussingers lived at the time. It will not be reproduced here as the location is private property, and the current occupants of the land have not been contacted. I was unable to travel to Vidor to inspect the area. Plugging the address into Google maps however provides an image captured by one of the infamous camera cars in 2011.

---

[26] I have been unable to confirm or deny if the Bussingers ever returned to the property after that night, nor if the Orange County Sheriff's Department followed through on their promise in the article to complete a follow up investigation. It occurred to me too late while writing this book that a Freedom of Information Act request to the Orange County Sheriff's Department and the Vidor Substation might shed additional light on the case, or at least confirm whether the investigation was completed. If nothing else, a copy of the police report from June 19, 1978, would make for engrossing reading. The request has been submitted and results are pending. Future editions of this book will provide updates should anything be found.

The Bussinger property, located at ▮▮▮▮▮▮▮▮ in Vidor, TX in 2011. Current owners unknown. Image taken from Google Maps.

There is a house on the property, though it is impossible to say if it is the same house that was present in 1978. The presence of a window air conditioning unit however would seem to indicate that the building is not of contemporary design. Almost all modern builds in Texas have central air.

There is a driveway connected to the road and a thick tree line. Deputy Reeves' statement that the creature stood at the boundary of the woods "fifty yards" from the edge of the driveway would seem feasible. Even accounting for erosion, natural growth of the tree line, and the possible replacement or refurbishment of the architectural fixtures, the location lends itself to the sequence of events detailed in Rice's original article.

Staring long at the trees, one can pick out two or more locations which may be specific to: "It was between two small oaks that form a vee," although this may be true of any thick wood line. Nonetheless, the account of the

Vidor Werewolf provides a fascinating study in cryptid encounters, and further research is undoubtedly warranted.

Much to my surprise and glee, there are two more tales in this corner of the Triangle. One is an anecdotal Dogman encounter out of Orange County, TX. In the "Southern Werewolves" episode of Lyle Blackburn's podcast *Monstro Bizarro,* Mr. Blackburn relays a sequence of events he received from fellow researcher and author Nick Redfern. This encounter is far more supernatural than many of the others covered, involving a haunting green mist which seemed to emanate from the wolfish animal seen by the witness. This one is an interesting contrast with most other Texan werewolf sightings, which primarily seem to consist of appearances by strange animals, not supernatural beings.

And yet, that is how the story goes.

18

The Orange Shapeshifter - Orange, Texas - 1933

This encounter, mentioned in the preceding chapter, was recorded by veteran researcher, investigator, and paranormal author Nick Redfern. It appears that it was first shared with the public in the 2010 book *Monsters of Texas*, by Nick Redfern and Ken Gerhard, but also appears online, and was recently covered on *Monstro Bizarro. Monsters of Texas* contains a variety of interesting cases - some of which are mentioned in this volume - and covers every type of Texan monster imaginable. We have been unable to dive into Thunderbirds, Dinosaurs and Lake Monsters (to name a few) during this exploration, but Gerhard and Redfern cover every corner of the map, relentlessly rooting out every subspecies of cryptid in the state and profiling them in detail. The book is recommended (see: essential) reading to enjoyers of this volume.

A witness named Solomon reported to Mr. Redfern that he had witnessed an odd, upright creature that he could only describe as (what else?) a werewolf, near the town of Orange, Texas. Orange is just a few miles away from Vidor and sits adjacent to Port Arthur. The encounter took place in 1933. This makes it one of the earliest in the Triangle.

Port Arthur is yet another place in Texas with a strange and confounding legacy. The city was established by Arthur Edward Stillwell in 1895 as a coastal trade port and a stop along the Texas coast, heading towards Louisiana. Stillwell himself was a captivating individual. He was a devout spiritualist and would later write in his 1921 book *Live and Grow Old* that he had been receiving messages from non-corporeal entities since childhood, which he referred to as "Brownies." Apparently, they directed him to found the city of Port Arthur, as well as told him who he would marry before he had met the woman. They advised him in various enterprises throughout his very successful life.

Orange, Texas is the location of the seat of Orange County. Founded sometime before 1830, it was first called Green's Bluff, then Madison, and finally Orange in 1958, six years after becoming the county seat. It is a mix of coastal land and Texas wilderness, depending upon the area one frequents.

When he was a boy, Solomon was fishing with two friends in a wooded area near the town in question. They were idling away the day next to a shallow stream with which they were familiar, when all three children were stricken with an uncanny sense of dread. This feeling of being watched is described by other witnesses in appearances of odd, unidentifiable life forms.

The sighting started as a large wolf head poking through the tree line on the opposite shore. This would be enough to frighten most children, but the subject continued to crawl forth from the underbrush, bringing its whole body into focus. Solomon tells Mr. Redfern that the creature was "around ten feet long," and mentions a particularly muscular build (yet another thing repeatedly mentioned by witnesses in these incidents).

The beast paced the bank in front of them, while they apparently watched in stunned silence. Whether the boys were captivated by the animal or too scared to react is not specified. After a time, the wolf-being sat on its haunches, and Solomon claims that it then began to "quickly vibrate," and uses the descriptors, "wrong and horrible." An odd, green tinted mist began to rise from the ground beneath the wolf's feet. As the "vibration" of the thing's body subsided, something even stranger occurred.

By now, we are familiar with this aspect of the story. The creature stood, slowly, rising from its haunches onto its hind legs. It then turned away and walked on two paws into the forest.

Should this be interpreted as an instance of shapeshifting, or simply a Dogman moving from a crouch to standing? Some would argue a more likely explanation is that Solomon saw a mundane wolf, the type not quite yet extirpated from Texas in the year 1933, and that his childhood memories may have become skewed in the intervening decades. Nick Redfern wrote in 2010 that he had interviewed Solomon, "a couple of years ago." If the incident occurred in 1933, that is approximately a 77-year gap between Solomon's encounter and his interview with Mr. Redfern. This is a lot of time in which to misremember something.

However, the age of a story does not disqualify it as a legitimate encounter. Every person alive has watershed moments in their life that they remember with absolute clarity and will never forget. The question also comes up again: *why? Why make something like this up? Why stand by the story for almost 80 years? Why go on record in a print publication and allow a renowned author to relay your experience if it was something you invented as a child?*

To be fair, one might also ask, *why not?*

But this event, taking place in such proximity to not only strange Port Arthur, but also werewolf-infested Vidor, should not be omitted from the investigation at hand. Ignoring the fact that Orange quite literally is the border that divides Texas from Louisiana, the Sabine River sits at the city's edge. If one attempted to ford it, they would find themselves in Creole Country. This area is known as the home of the dire and unknowable Rougarou, Louisiana's own bipedal canine.

It has been previously noted that there are three sightings of this sort in the area. The most recent took place in 2022 and comes from yet another independent witness unaware of similar goings on within the territory.

19

Road Crossing in Conroe, TX - 2022

Killian Geisser was born in Germany and did not run into much cryptozoological lore during his childhood. He now resides in the United States and on June 29th of 2022 joined the growing list of witnesses of the strangeness of Texas. I was introduced to Killian by Joe Doyle of Hellbent Holler, after Killian had posted a comment on one of the Hellbent Holler *Werewolf Experiments* investigations on YouTube, stating that he had seen something similar in southern Texas. Not only that, but the sighting was incredibly recent. Joe contacted me right away, and within a few hours Killian had relayed his story and agreed to its inclusion in the Texas Dogman Triangle.

"I just shared a weird encounter of mine on the Hellbent Holler YouTube channel, and they asked me to reach out to you, to tell you about it," his email began.

"Just a little side note to the whole thing, I'm originally from Germany and I didn't grow up knowing anything about these beings. I never cared about the subject, and I never researched anything about this.

"That was until June 29th, this year. I was on a road trip with my family, just passing through Texas, coming from New Mexico. My brother was sitting in the passenger seat right next to me and he saw the same thing. Our trip went by Lake Conroe on 105 and the whole thing happened between Conroe and Ainsworth, TX."

As I have done with other reports, I searched out the location online and browsed through some of the available satellite imagery. The territory around Highway 105 seems to be equal parts developed and undeveloped, with plenty of tree cover and greenbelts which run to the north and south between regular residential and business districts. Once again, despite a heavy human presence, there is plenty of room for something monstrous to hide. In addition, Lake Conroe is yet another water source adjacent to one of these "unbelievable" reports.

"We were maybe going around 50 mph at the time, and I was just chatting with my brother, but when I looked back onto the road, there was a big, hairy, brown being, crossing the road about 100-150 yards in front of us. It was noon and broad daylight." In a later email Killian would specify that "It was around 1:30 pm and bright sunshine. Extremely hot too."

The temperature around Conroe in June of 2022 averaged a steamy 91 degrees Fahrenheit, and the weather calendars I consulted show a bright, yellow sun on almost every day of the month. By now the reader will have noticed that these animals or beings or monsters seem mostly to be active at night, making Killian's sighting of particular interest. Thankfully, Killian had the advantage of daylight to aid in his report.

"Although there was another car coming up ahead, that thing was just absolutely relaxed. It was not running or anything. It was casually walking. What puzzled me the most was that even though it was walking, it cleared the road at an incredible speed. It walked right into the woods and once it reached the tree line it completely disappeared. The people who were coming towards us on the other side of the road were just as puzzled. I can't say that it was 9 feet tall or something like that, but my guess would be around 7 feet. What was more shocking than the height was the overall size of the thing. Massive shoulders and massive arms. Now I don't know what category that would fit in... was that a Dogman? A Sasquatch? To me it looked more like what I would imagine a Sasquatch to look like. It had a weird head though."

In a series of emails, I asked Killian to describe any distinctive physical features. I was careful not to mention pointed ears or yellow eyes.

"The look of it was simply a very very large and muscular man covered in brown hair. The head was shaped in a weird way, and almost pointy, which actually could've been ears, now that I think of it. The head was a darker colour than the body. Almost black. The body had the same brown colour as a grizzly bear. It walked upright like a human."[27]

"The odd part about it was the feeling that we got when it crossed. It felt like it wanted us to see it and after it disappeared it felt like it said, *'now you've seen me.'* If that was a guy in a suit, then it was the biggest, fastest and strongest human on the planet lol! So that's my story."[28]

"I remember feeling an incredible rush of adrenaline when it appeared. I actually yelled out *'WTF IS THAT.'* That's when my brother saw it. Here comes the odd thing, I was not feeling any kind of fear. It was just adrenaline and disbelief. The strongest feeling I felt was that the being showed itself to us because it wanted us to see it. My brother did not feel that, he was just shocked. To me it felt like it basically said *'Here I am, and I want you to look at me.'"*

---

[27] The European spelling of "colour" has been intentionally included, per Killian's statement.

[28] Killian did not seek financial compensation for his testimony. He did not seek me out or try to insert himself into an existing narrative. He simply shared an experience he could not explain, and in return asked only that I notify him when this book became available for purchase. I was more than happy to oblige.

This is odd indeed, and not just due to the nature of the sighting itself. Most witnesses in these cases describe a powerful sense of fear at the sight of the monsters, as we have discussed. This lack of terror might indicate that this sighting differs from others we have examined. However, the physical description of a muscular upper body and pointed ears harken to tales told by other witnesses who implicitly use the term "werewolf."

Yet another piece of a very, very strange puzzle.

Beyond the Triangle

While many of the cases examined in this book take place within the Texas Dogman Triangle 'proper' (see the Maps section of this work for visual definitions of these boundaries), there is a wealth of evidence and anecdotes coming from well outside its edges. Some anecdotal encounters could not be confirmed or researched and have been omitted. Some, however, provided both documentation and/or photographic evidence, and/or come from a reliable source and as such, have been included. They may also simply correlate to the locations of other, better documented sightings, and are mentioned due largely to proximity.

Rather than redraw the lines of the Triangle to arbitrarily include them, these encounters have been simply categorized as Beyond the Triangle.

20

Werewolves of the Border - San Benito, McAllen, Bluetown - 1990s-2013

San Benito

A particularly interesting case covered on the *True Horror Stories of Texas* website is that of the San Benito Encounter. Jon Gonzalez and his team were the first to break this story, as it was shared with them by the original witness. Like some other reports in this book, it cannot necessarily be stated definitively that this is a true Dogman encounter. It fits the profile of many strange humanoid sightings, occurring from an appreciable distance in an isolated place. What separates it from innumerable other "strange humanoid" sightings is that it takes place during broad daylight, like Killian's sighting. It is captured on video. It is both witnessed and remarked upon by more than one person.

In addition, what is unequivocally certain is that *something* alive and quite possibly inhuman appears in the video, and the witness has made no attempt to "cash in" on the report in the almost ten years since it was filmed. It was shared by Jon Gonzalez in 2019 in an article titled *Dog-like Humanoid Creature* but was originally filmed in 2013.

"Of course, you know the rules of filming anything paranormal. It's gotta be the worst quality, you've gotta shake as much as you can." Jon said when I interviewed him in 2022.

The video is shot from a body of water, a small lake according to the description. The far bank of the lake is in the center frame, and the vegetation is lush, bright green. About halfway through the minute and 12-second-long clip, a blurry brown shape can be seen crouching over the water. At first it appears to be a rock, cluster of vegetation or perhaps a tree stump, but at 53 seconds the figure rises - into an upright, bipedal stance. At first glance the witness, a man named Reuben, and his friend (who is not named) thought the animal was a dog or similar species until the great reveal. Reuben's reactions are captured on the audio, and despite constant interference from the wind whipping into the microphone, his tone seems to indicate genuine amazement.

"What the f***... so it's something... a dog or what?"

When the creature stands, Reuben exclaims,

"A la verga* ... oh sh***... !"[29]

The video continues to roll, but the hairy brown figure disappears into the underbrush.

"I got it on video, ay?" Reuben says, before the clip terminates at 1:12.

A still frame captured from the original video hosted on True Horror Stories of Texas, used with permission

---

[29] *Spanish pejorative

The obvious arguments used in the debunking of strange videos apply here, some of which are mentioned by Jon Gonzales. The video is shot from far away. The picture is unclear. The audio is of poor quality. It could be a person in a costume. It could just be a person. It could be some kind of hoax, etc.

What it almost certainly cannot be is a classified species of wildlife native to the Texas/Mexico border. There are no known primates, which is another close description, indigenous to the American Southwest. Once again, we must make the comparison to Sasquatch sightings.

In the witnesses' favor is their near anonymity - no television appearances, no book deals, no viral TikTok videos. The report has also remained on the *True Horror Stories of Texas* website without excessive fanfare. If this is an attempt at a hoax, it is one with a distinct lack of advertising. There are no "San Benito Werewolf" or "San Benito Sasquatch" or "Scruffy San Benito Lake Man" T-shirts to be found online and the city has not, to date, opened a monster museum. Whether this lends credibility to the sighting (or makes no difference) is left to the interpretation of the viewer. Some comments left on the original article criticize the witness for already recording when the odd figure appears, but this is not an uncommon habit for any sportsmen. An angler cannot know when a catch will occur, and the only way to film one is to have the camera rolling.

I asked Jeremiah Byron, previously quoted in this volume, for his opinion on the video.

"The way they react is extremely interesting. The one gentleman laughs in surprise when the creature stands up, and it's the type of laughter that comes when you've seen something you can't explain. It can't be faked."

"That video I posted, it went viral. It went super viral." Jon Gonzales said of the clip in 2022. It was picked up by other websites, including radio and news stations, and was hotly discussed in the back alleys of Reddit and Facebook.

Bluetown

Comments left on the original article may indicate the presence of additional strange activity in this area. One user posted in response:

"I wouldn't be so quick to discredit it. I've seen a creature like that once before. It was back in the early 90's. I was driving down Military Highway, somewhere between Bluetown and Los Indios. It was about one o'clock in the morning. I noticed a couple of cars ahead of me had swerved toward the middle of the road. It looked like they were trying to avoid something. As I got closer, my friend and I noticed something very big and tall walking along the side of the road. I slowed down a little and honked my horn. It turned and looked toward us. We couldn't believe what we saw. My friend thought it was just a guy in a suit or something. But its eyes were shining in the headlights. And I know human eyes don't shine in the light. Only animal's eyes shine when light hits their eyes. I've heard stories of people who live in that area that claim to have seen a creature like a Bigfoot or Sasquatch around the Rio Grande River and the Resacas... I never believed them until I saw it for myself."

Bluetown, Texas is only twenty miles southwest of San Benito, a bit closer to Mexico and the Rio Grande. The story in the comment may be fiction, but if so, it is fiction written by someone familiar with the area - or, perhaps, someone with too much spare time and access to Google maps. After being shared as a comment, Jon shared the encounter as a separate posting on the website. Once again, there is a mention of Sasquatch sightings sitting closely on the map to what may be a Dogman encounter.

McAllen

Moving even further west there is yet another anecdotal encounter shared on *True Horror Stories of Texas*. This one took place in McAllen, Texas in 2008 - seventy miles from San Benito and the unidentified form captured on camera, and only fifty miles from Bluetown.

While driving a friend home sometime between ten PM and midnight, the witness reports seeing another vehicle driving erratically further down the road, apparently attempting to avoid some yet unseen obstacle. The passengers of the witness's vehicle - friend Eric, the witness's sister, and her boyfriend - collectively reported seeing "a huge dog that looked like a black great Dane."

The beast "stood straight up on two feet and walked slowly in front of both cars as he was staring directly at our (Chevrolet) Blazer."

Upon reaching the sidewalk on the far side of 29th street, the thing "Got on all fours and headed west toward Ware Road."

Regarding the description, the witness recounts: "I personally didn't see the thing, but my friend said it was almost identical to the werewolf in *Harry Potter: The Prisoner of Azkaban*. Tall, skinny, pitch black & very fast."

Sadly, this encounter does not include photographic evidence. It does, however, fit the continuing profile of odd canid sightings which we have come to associate with suspected Dogman encounters. The beast was seen at night, on a roadway, and moved from a quadrupedal to a bipedal stance before disappearing. This behavior is recurring. The creature, at first appearing to be a normal, if not overly large, dog rising to stand on two legs when confronted. The sightings mentioned in previous chapters repeatedly involve these animals rising from all fours onto two feet.

Is this behavior some kind of intimidation tactic? An example of an animal trying to make itself appear bigger? Many animals will perform what is called a "bluff charge" to scare away potential assailants and avoid a physical confrontation. Might this "standing up" habit of the strange canines be something similar?

The Texas/Mexico border is an area steeped in paranormal folklore. While interviewing contributors for an episode of *Hey Strangeness* concerning the dreaded La Lechuza, Sara and I were told by two separate witnesses with no connection to each other that they had, in their lifetimes, witnessed what they believed to be a living La Lechuza, or Witch Owl, near or just over the Mexican Border. This is but one example.

This area also contains widespread talk of the Chupacabra, The Texas Terror Dog, La Llorona and even mention of doppelgängers, UFOs, and Men in Black. These elements are sometimes closely intermixed with Christian beliefs (most often Catholic), and the mythology of this area very often can be traced to traditional cautionary tales told to children, passed down by countless generations.

Here there is no moral lesson - simply a strange series of encounters in the far south of Texas near the Mexican border. During my interview with Joedy Cook of the North American Dogman Project, he relayed an anecdote about a witness who had contacted him while working for the United States Border Patrol. This anonymous officer claimed to have unequivocally seen Dogmen, or werewolves, on numerous occasions near the Mexican border. He said that in some cases they had been known to kill human beings. He and his fellow patrol officers were told in no uncertain terms to keep quiet about their sightings and not to pursue or otherwise engage with these animals.

For reasons of privacy, I was unable to learn this witness's name or contact them. Regardless, the disclosed location of this purported activity does correlate with the geography of the other three incidents detailed in this chapter. Once again, independent witnesses with no connection to one another other than geography report strange and dangerous wolf creatures in the desert.

Watchers of the weird would do well to keep an eye on the southern border of Texas.

21

A Werewolf(?) in Greggton - Greggton, Texas – 1958

Greggton was established in 1873. Originally named Willow Springs and founded as a station along the Texas and Pacific Railway.

My first introduction to this story came via the *True Horror Stories of Texas* website, in an article written by Jon Gonzalez. There are other blogs, forum posts, and comment threads summarizing the tale, but Mr. Gonzales' article was the first one I read, and his summary of the story is succinct.

Mrs. Delburt Gregg, a resident of Greggton, Texas reports one night seeing a large, terrifying visage fitting the description of a werewolf outside her window. The creature fled into the bushes, and when it reappeared, it would seem to have changed shape. The terrifying encounter would, in a way, slip between the cracks of Texas' oral history. This obscure tale has finally resurfaced, due to the recent shot-in-the-arm that interest in Dogman encounters has begun to receive over the last few years. Since then, it has appeared in numerous online articles, podcasts, and other content. The complete text of Mrs. Gregg's encounter originally appeared on pages 60 and 61 of the March 1960 edition of *Fate* magazine.[30]

Mrs. Delburt Gregg's description of the intruder on her land begins with the title of her letter - *"Werewolf?"* -

---

[30] There were numerous references online to "an article in *Fate* magazine," but I was unable to find a scan or transcript. At long last I broke down, ordered a copy of the magazine on eBay, and joyfully confirmed the story's source.

and she summarizes her encounter as a "strange experience" taking place in July of 1958. Her husband was away on business, and Mrs. Gregg dozed by an open window to catch a wash of cool air from an approaching storm. It was hot in July of 1958, with median temperatures averaging in the 80s and 90s in that part of the country. The cool air of a stormfront would offer certain reprieve from the dense summer heat of eastern Texas. Greggton sits less than fifty miles from the border of Louisiana, a place notorious for its humidity, and the climate is a feature the two states share. Tales of upright walking wolves (recall the dreaded Rougarou) are another.

Mrs. Gregg was "awakened with a start" to the sound of scratching noises coming from the window screen she lay next to. Moments passed, and as the storm rolled in, a flash of lighting illuminated a monstrous profile in the darkened window.

"I grasped [sic] in horror. A huge, shaggy, wolf-like creature was clawing at the screen and staring at me with baleful, glowing slitted eyes. I could see its bared white fangs."

Reflexively, Mrs. Gregg seized a flashlight from her nightstand as she sprung from the bed. Turning to face the window she activated the torch, and caught another glimpse of the thing as it, "fled away from the window, across the yard into a thick clump of bushes near the highway."

She watched the thickly packed underbrush, waiting for the beastly thing to re-emerge, perhaps newly emboldened after being shocked from the fog of sleep. Curiosity surely played a role. What exactly had she seen?

However, "after a time" what emerged from the brush was not a wolf, but the unmistakable form of a tall, upright human man. The man "walked hurriedly down the road, disappearing into the darkness." Mrs. Delburt Gregg secured and locked the open window, then slept fitfully with the lights on until morning.

This encounter bears close aesthetic resemblance to more traditional "Hollywood" werewolf stories, with an implied animal-to-human transformation occurring on a stormy night. Three American films were released in the 50s with werewolf-centric content - *The Werewolf* in 1956, *I Was a Teenage Werewolf* in 1957, and *How to Make a Monster* (released on July 1st of 1958 - the same year and month as Mrs. Delburt Gregg's reported encounter). The seminal classic *The Wolf Man* starring Lon Chaney Jr. and Bela Lugosi had premiered in 1941, several years removed from the Greggton encounter, but still likely within the realm of common knowledge.

It should be stated that *How to Make a Monster* was not truly a "werewolf movie" but features a rather strange plot wherein a makeup artist hypnotizes actors in-costume, forcing them to commit horrible acts of violence. One of the villain's puppet-like victims is dressed as a werewolf. The chronological juxtaposition of the films with Mrs. Gregg's encounter does not prove falsification or fancy but is worth mentioning. Could Mrs. Gregg have been disoriented in her half-asleep state and confused an ordinary animal for a bipedal canine? Could familiarity with pop culture depictions of werewolves at the time have played a subconscious role in her perception of what happened? Could she have simply had a very vivid dream which she later mistook for reality? Or - inversely - does this sighting fit the already established and oft repeated profile of Dogman/werewolf sightings in Texas?

Sketch of a Sleeping Dogman by Mike Garcia

Whether Mrs. Gregg had seen or was aware of these or any other werewolf films is unknown, but there must certainly be an origin for her point of reference. It is possible that the title - *"Werewolf?"* - was an invention of the editors of *Fate*, and not the witness's original title given that the term werewolf appears nowhere within the text, but this is pure speculation. The story is an entertaining one, and its location on the map of Texas places it within reasonable proximity to not only other potential Dogman encounters, but also areas with a dense concentration of Sasquatch reports. In a straight line, Greggton is only about

70 miles from Fouke, Arkansas - the location of the (ongoing) Boggy Creek Monster saga, one of the best documented Sasquatch cases in the last century.[31]

Permission was also sought from *Fate* magazine to include the original text of this article in The Texas Dogman Triangle. To my knowledge the article has never been reproduced outside of the 1960 magazine, and as my own search validated, it is not available anywhere online at time of writing. Heather Moser, whose assistance in the writing of this book has been invaluable, was able to reach someone at *Fate*.

Below, and with the permission of *Fate* Magazine, is Mrs. Delburt Gregg's own story, included without alteration, and in print for the first time (as far as we are aware) since 1960.

Werewolf?

By Mrs. Delburt Gregg

This strange experience happened to me one night last July in 1958, when my husband was away on business. I had pushed my bed close to a large window hoping to catch the cool breeze from a thunder storm which was gathering on the southwestern horizon. It was stifling hot and I couldn't seem to rest. But I snapped off the bed light and lay quietly trying to go to sleep.

---

[31] Attempts to contact modern relatives of Mrs. Delburt Gregg have proven unsuccessful, and inquiries sent to local agencies in the Greggton area likely to be connected with local historians have thus far gone unanswered. Perhaps more background regarding this story will emerge as interest in it grows, but for now it remains an interesting footnote, nestled in a hotspot of other alleged paranormal activity.

Finally I dozed off. How long I slept I do not know, but I awakened with a start. A faint scratching sound was coming from the screened window beside my face. I lay still staring at the screen window as the seconds ticked by. Suddenly a bright flash of lightning lit up the window for an instant. I grasped in horror. A huge, shaggy, wolf-like creature was clawing at the screen and glaring at me with baleful, glowing, slitted eyes. I could see its bared white fangs.

I grabbed my flash light from the table nearby and leaped from the bed. Then I shot the beam of light toward the window in time to catch another glimpse of the monstrous animal as it fled away from the open window, across the yard into a thick clump of bushes near the highway.

I watched for the animal to come out of the bushes but, after a short time, instead of a shaggy wolf running out, the figure of an extremely tall man suddenly parted the thick foliage and walked hurriedly off down the road, disappearing into the darkness.

Cold prickles of fear ran over me. I closed the window and locked it; and I slept with a bright light on in my room the rest of that night.

- *Greggton, Tex*

22

Roscoe (Multiple incidents, dates unknown)

In the spirit of full disclosure, details around these events and reports of Dogman activity in this area are scant. Consideration was given to omitting this story, but Roscoe sits only fifty miles down Interstate 20 from another important location: Abilene. To ignore a potential connection to Abilene was unthinkable, even if it is only a coincidental geographical one. The reason for this is an altogether different phenomenon.

Home of the Black-Eyed Kids

In recent years, paranormal enthusiasts have hotly discussed the Black-Eyed Kids, or BEKs, also called the Black-Eyed Children. This phenomenon is yet another that we will mention here without the proper space to fully document or explore in any depth. It suffices to say that BEKs are as much a part of the strangeness of Texas as the Dogman encounters which are the topic of this volume, the long history of Sasquatch reports, and the odd glow of the Marfa Lights. The story – or stories, as purported encounters are now beyond legion – goes that a strange looking child or pair of children will request entrance into a person's home or automobile, usually under the guise of asking for help.

Strange looking may be an understatement. The children are universally described as pale with gaunt features and most terrifying of all, jet black eyes (if one could not guess by the name). The witnesses are consistently stricken with terror, and the few examples in which the BEKs are admitted entrance are said to end in tragedy. What these beings are, where they come from, and what they want is the topic of countless debates.

The first interaction with the BEKs was reported by journalist Brian Bethel in 1996. News began to spread, and the not-quite-human entities first gained widespread recognition when the case was picked up by paranormal author and researcher David Weatherly.

David is one of the pillars of the paranormal field, and early in his career corresponded with the legendary John Keel. David literally wrote the book on the Black-Eyed Kids in 2012 with cover art by the visionary Mister Sam Shearon. In a 2022 interview for my show *Strange Conversations*, he stated that he still receives sporadic reports from experiencers of these terrifying meetings. In his 2012 book, *Black Eyed Children*, David makes comparisons to everything from alien hybrids to demonic entities and then some.

The first report of the BEKs, documented in 1996 by Brian Bethal, took place in Abilene. This has forever cemented the city's legacy as a place of dire strangeness. Even before the uncanny appearance of these otherworldly youngsters the city had a supernatural history, keeping in step with many other overly haunted Texas cities and towns. There is far more here to discuss, of course, but we risk deviating too greatly from the topic at hand.

A Series of Misadventures

A few dozen miles away from the city of Abilene, a witness reports multiple sightings of a Dogman-like creature. The dates of these events are not given, and the only indication we are provided regarding the passage of time is a mention of "eight years later when I was a sophomore in highschool." Neither provided are the name of the reporting witness, the names of most of the additional experiencers they claim to be affiliated with, nor the specific locations such as crossroads or national parks. This makes it virtually impossible to assess the potential veracity of this sequence of events.[32]

The witness reports their first encounter taking place during childhood. Alone in their bedroom, which faced a nearby stretch of woods, they saw something which would frighten anyone, never mind a young child.

"It had yellow eyes, long snout of a dog, black fur, it face is kinda human subtract the snout and the gnarly long teeth, and fur all over its face, once it realized I noticed it, it snarled at me quietly through the window and it was a stare down. I slowly pulled the covers over my head. I then proceeded to cry for what felt like forever, then I ran into my parents room crying. Telling me it was just a dream."[33]

The witness goes on to say that eight years passed, and when they were roughly at the age of a high school sophomore, they went on a fishing trip in an isolated area with a group of friends. Another disturbing wildlife encounter would occur, but this one would be experienced

---

[32] Since so little of this story can be verified, I considered omitting it from the text, primarily for fear of attracting ridicule. However, exploration of the paranormal often leads to ridicule, and to exclude what may be a credible sighting or even sequence of them due to a personal hang-up feels grossly irresponsible. Besides, once you have repeatedly said out loud to your associates and loved ones, "werewolves are real," the metric for potential criticism has long since been redefined. In addition, and to their credit, the reporting source of these encounters is the database of the now well-known North American Dogman Project.

[33] A quick reminder: As with many of the other excerpts in this book, the text of the original report has been presented as it is available to the public without alteration, save minor changes to capitalization, spelling, and punctuation.

by the witness's brother. Joe (the brother's name) left the place where he was fishing by himself to relieve himself in the nearby woods. When he returned, he found what he described as "more of a Bigfoot" feasting on a jar of peanut butter that Joe had brought along with him. He ran back to the others, hysterical, but was not believed. He was dubbed Crazy Joey for his efforts. Oddly, Joe or Crazy Joey is the only individual given a name in this report.

Most people are not fortunate enough - or misfortunate enough, depending upon who you ask - to have even a single inexplicable experience in their lives, let alone two. Joey would cross paths with the same monster again, however, after returning to the same spot for another fishing trip, this one a solo venture. On this outing a bird became tangled in his line, and he witnessed the same bipedal creature attempting to catch the unfortunate avian. There is some verbiage about him running home, retrieving a knife, and trying to cut the bird loose, but the syntax of the telling is a bit difficult to decipher. To be specific:

"He was catching some fish, his line was all screwed up and took it off his fishing and re-spooled it he ran come because he only had one hook on the pole. He ran back and claimed he the same thing chasing the bird that was wrapped up, he yelled scared it, then ran back home for knife as fast as he can, then cut it free."

Even after these incidents occurred, more activity is reported. On another undated fishing trip, the witness caught sight of what looked like a "gray wolf" which, while on all fours, came up to their waist. The witness describes themself as being of average height, roughly, 5'6". They then made attempts to frighten the beast away.

"I started walking and saw what I thought to be a big grey wolf easily waist me being 5.6? Anythings possible, my friend got cornered by 4 coyotes out there once. But sure enough, the creature by another giant oak tree and I made eye contact again another stare down only different since it was on all fours. It was obviously interested in my friends since it was following the trail that leads there, I yelled and chased it, the look on its face was playful because it was probably pretending not to notice me, so I chased it to the clearing, the retention ponds are on the left and a small prairie on the right."

Once again, the flow of the narrative becomes jumbled by the verbiage, but the story would seem to go that the witness left the presence of the animal to return to where the rest of their friends were fishing.

The witness then specifically states, "Sure enough I quickly forgot when one my friends caught a pig of large mouth that weighed 3 1/2 pounds on the first cast. I waited until we were going to leave to inform them because I didn't want ruin the fact we were catching bass on every cast."

Shortly after the group was told to leave the area by a private security guard, as they were unknowingly trespassing. Still, the report goes on:

"The last time we saw something similar, Me and My brother were scavenging for roadkill when saw a Black dog/maybe it look at us ran away constantly back, it moved gracefully through the brush, meanwhile me and my brother were absolutely getting torn up by the razz berry bushes. We catch up, it waits, then runs away again, we played this game 5 times with that thing, then we couldn't find it again."[34]

---

[34] Once again, this excerpt is presented largely in its original format. I will reserve comment on the act of scavenging for roadkill, but I am acquainted with at least one creator who uses scavenged bones as an art

The witness is nothing if not open minded. In a single report they attribute five separate incidents to potential Dogman or strange canine sightings. The stories are relayed in a format which one might describe as a stream of consciousness.

The first story would seem to have the most detailed description. The ears, eyes, and teeth are all in focus, and the witness recalls them vividly. Once more, we see a recurrence of the yellow eyes, as well as other facial features consistent in Dogman reports. The "human" features mentioned remind one of the alleged shapeshifters of Greggton seen in 1958, though this element does not seem to be present in the majority of the reported sightings in the state.

The second and third stories are second-hand accounts, but both coming from the same associate of the person making the report.

Two problems arise in examination of these stories. First, the witness states that Crazy Joey was off fishing by himself, apart from the rest of the group, when he left his pole and peanut butter to relieve himself on the other side of the creek. Why he crossed the creek to urinate when he was already alone is not specified.

Next, in the third encounter Crazy Joey returns to the site to confirm his sighting, even though in the first story he is described as terrified and hysterical after seeing the strange "Bigfoot" like creature. Why he would return after experiencing such intense fright (unaccompanied no less) is also not specified. The succession of events involving the fishing line, the bird, and his attempt to free

---

medium. There may be other reasons for this activity, but it is probably not any of my business.

said bird is also confusing, but this does not necessarily detract from the veracity of the story.

The fourth sighting is admittedly of a creature on all fours. Depending on the year in which it took place, it is not out of scope for a surviving Gray Wolf or large Mexican Red Wolf specimen to be lurking around the Roscoe area. It is the reported behavior of the animal which is odd, and the witness's response to that behavior is even more so.

Why withhold from a group of friends that they are in very close proximity to a large, likely dangerous animal? Are a few choice fish worth one's life and limb? Or is the presence of large and abundant fish truly so exciting that one will "forget" that they have just encountered an enormous wolf-like thing stalking their companions? I would argue that they are not, but to each his own.

It is not my intent to lampoon this account. The usual question of "why bother making this up?" applies here. Also, the lack of polish in the witness's writing could indicate an ordinary person not concerned with flowery language, only wanting to relay a succession of strange experiences. There are also several seemingly insignificant details in the text ("I felt alone after 12 minutes then I took my bag, 2 poles, and tackle") which, if imagined, are oddly specific.

Another thing working to the witness's credit is the environment surrounding Roscoe. Wide open spaces, a healthy supply of prairie and farmland, and enough vegetation to hide if a person or animal were particularly sneaky. Abilene State Park is but a stone's throw (forty miles) from Roscoe and made up of over five hundred acres. Depending upon the time frame the witness is referencing, these areas may have been far less developed and isolated when the sightings took place.

It is not the writer's charge to determine whether a report is legitimate, nonetheless, to not filter these accounts through the mesh of skepticism is a dangerous path. Blind belief invites hoaxers and shysters by the dozen to appropriate the research of cryptozoologists and spin it for their own gain. It's been done before (in some cases very recently) and will certainly be done again.

It can be assumed that the witness probably did see *something* at some point in their life, but with such limited information further deduction becomes much more difficult.

The Amarillo Dogman - Amarillo, Texas – 2022

Amarillo is in the northern portion of Texas, commonly referred to by locals and those in-the-know as the Panhandle. Closer to Albuquerque than to Dallas, Amarillo is nearly eight hours by car from the capital city of Austin. In jest, a friend of mine once referred to the Panhandle as south Oklahoma, though I would hesitate to make the joke in the presence of anyone from the northern region.

Hoax or Genuine Sighting?

In June of 2022 "Amarillo Texas" began to pop up in the top tens of various news aggregators, viral content circulators, and, for our purposes, paranormal blogs, websites, and social media accounts. While previously known as being home to a popular stop along the storied Route 66, as well as the location of the Don Harrington Discovery Center, an enchanting and well-loved space museum, this recent uptick in the city's popularity would be due to an altogether different animal - literally.

Somewhere around the early part of the month a thread emerged on Reddit, the birthplace of many viral sensations, containing a photo purported to be captured at "a zoo in Amarillo, Texas." The photo - shown below - seemed to showcase an upright walking creature with canine attributes.

The "Amarillo Dogman" - photo credit City of Amarillo, Texas -
https://www.amarillo.gov/Home/Components/News/News/2273/16

Since the case emerged while I was deep in the
throes of research for this very book, to not include it
seemed like a criminal waste of an opportunity. I followed
a news article sent by a friend to what I believed to be the
original Reddit thread which broke the story. Attempting to
contact the OP proved fruitless. From there, I sent inquiries
to various entities affiliated with the city of Amarillo itself -
Fish and Wildlife, Parks and Recreation, the Amarillo Zoo,
and City Hall seeking an interview, or at the very least, a
quote or comment. My inquiries went unreturned, and the
silence was deafening.

While this means nothing in and of itself, my mind
fabricated two potential conspiracies as the cause of the
brush off. Either these various organizations had been
advised not to speak to the media because the sighting was
legitimate and they wished to avoid a wave of attention
from paranormal thrill seekers, as has often been the case in
the past when similar sightings occurred elsewhere. Or, as a
nagging voice in the back of my mind began to repeat, they
had been advised not to speak to the media because the
sighting was part of a cleverly organized marketing
campaign and the powers-that-be wanted to prevent anyone
from spilling the beans.

It may very well be neither scenario. It is more likely that a few unsolicited emails from a self-styled "journalist" do not always warrant a response from over-worked and under-resourced public servants and/or employees of assorted organizations trying to do their jobs in an increasingly bizarre world. I would also learn later that I was not the only person sending inquiries to various Amarillo organizations asking for information, so my messages may well have simply been lost in the shuffle. However, if the scenario I conjured involving a marketing initiative was indeed the case, it would not be the first incident of its kind in recent memory. In fact, it would not even be the first such incident in Texas.

The Round Rock Saga

In 2017 a series of photos began circulating online, shared by the Round Rock Parks and Recreation department in Round Rock, Texas. The pictures - depicting footprints, strange looking clumps of hair, and broken tree branches - were said to have been taken by park rangers along various walking trails in several local parks. Old Settlers Park, Brushy Creek, and the Bull Creek Trails were among them. The Parks and Rec team in Round Rock capitalized on the budding popularity of the story, hosting an event called "Expedition: Find Bigfoot" at Old Settlers Park. Paranormal enthusiasts and initiates alike could attend the event for free, and for the negligible cost of $5 go on a guided "Expedition Walking Tour." A pair of burgeoning high school age outdoorsman/paranormal investigators even staged an overnight investigation in one of the parks in question, recording a few pieces of strange audio which they speculated might be the work of a Sasquatch.

A few days into the media buzz the Parks and Rec department also shared a video, depicting a dark, furry, bipedal creature fleeing into the woods away from the camera. The footage was in poor focus and shot from a great distance, just as we have seen with many videos of purported cryptid sightings. Nevertheless, the social media posts touting it claimed that it had been captured by a resident of Round Rock living along the Bull Creek Greenbelt.

Later investigation by a local journalist revealed what many had already come to suspect - the case was a hoax. The assorted photos had been shared on Bigfoot blogs and forums at various times over the years, and the video which had sparked such a sensation originated in Russia. The clip had been its own viral buzz a few years before, claimed by some to be a captured sighting of an *almasty* - a Russian term which roughly translates to Sasquatch, Yeti, or Bigfoot.

While some hardcore cryptozoologists would decry the falsehood perpetuated by the parks department, a general sentiment shared by many members of the community today is that the hoax was, at the very least, well intentioned. Young people became interested in the field of cryptozoology and some even undertook their own investigations. Families hunted for Bigfoot amidst the trails of Old Settlers Park, passing signs with monikers such as "Bigfoot Crossing," "Don't feed the Chupacabras," and "Beware the Loch Ness Monster."[35]

Two Investigations, Similar Conclusions

This case of a family-friendly and well-intentioned hoax came to mind shortly after I was initially shown the Amarillo Dogman photo. In an interesting twist, the initial "sightings" in Round Rock were reported in June of 2017,

---

[35] Also, a lot of people got some universally necessary exercise.

and the Expedition event was held in July of that year. Almost five years _to the date_ the Amarillo Dogman emerged, and the city of Amarillo posted a news item on their website requesting help identifying the "UAO - Unidentified Amarillo Object."

In my interview with author and investigator Michael Mayes of _Texas Cryptid Hunter_ and the North American Wood Ape Conservancy during the research phase of this book, I asked for his opinion on the Amarillo Dogman. Completely unprompted, he referenced the Round Rock Sasquatch case of 2017. We agreed that the two had traits in common but were not necessarily in sync with each other. We also acknowledged that without further information it would be nearly impossible to draw any sort of educated conclusion.

I was not at a complete dead end, however. Modern technology provides one with ample opportunities to think outside the box when it comes to obtaining relevant bits of data, regardless of one's topic of inquiry. I realized that the best way to research this case would be to put boots on the ground in Amarillo, interview locals, and examine the terrain. Several of my venerated and more accomplished colleagues have expressed the same thing. Sadly, my personal circumstances prevented such a journey at time of writing. In lieu of the eight-hour drive from Austin, I made a virtual exploration of the space around the Amarillo Zoo using Google Maps. One may jest at the superficial nature of the "armchair investigator," but this venture did provide one interesting clue.

The original "Amarillo Dogman" photo (above), image of the perimeter fencing at the Amarillo Zoo (below), taken from Google Maps.

The original photo shows a chain link fence roughly twice the height of the suspected cryptid. There is a Y shaped formation of barbed wire at the top, supported by metal posts spaced at regular intervals - perhaps 8 to 12 feet apart. Using Google Maps, I was able to capture an image of the perimeter fencing near the parking lot of the Amarillo Zoo - a very similar, if not identical arrangement to the structure shown in the photo captured by the stationary camera. This at the very least seemed to confirm the purported origins of the photo - The Amarillo Zoo - a sharp contrast to the evidence presented in 2017 during the Round Rock saga. One thing to note are the bits of debris caught in the fence in the second photo. Some researchers would posit that the Amarillo Dogman may be naught but a piece of trash, caught in the fence, flapping in the breeze, photographed over several moments by the slow exposure of the stationary camera.

Paranormal investigator Ashley Hilt, known on assorted social platforms by the shorthand Asherz, also took an interest in the case when it began making rounds. On July 21st of 2022, during a conversation on social networking platform Clubhouse, hosted by Greg Morrill, leader of the *Cryptocasters* discussion group on the topic of hoaxes, an audience member inquired after the Amarillo Dogman and asked for the opinion of the panel members. Asherz and I were both members of said panel, and all the better that it took place during the drafting of this manuscript. Asherz had made a few of her own inquiries into the case and discovered a few more bits of information that seemed neither to contradict nor complement my own.

She explains:

"It was recommended to me on Reddit. I won't say that I was the first investigator on the trail of this thing, but I do believe I was one of the first ones. At the time that I came across it, the name of the Facebook group hadn't even been disclosed yet. So, I waited impatiently. Eventually, the original poster of the Reddit thread dropped the holy grail. *ZooKreepers*. Cool. I now had something to work with. I hop onto Facebook and search it up. No *ZooKreepers*. Tons of *Zookreeper*-type pages. *ZOOKreepers: After Dark, Zoo, ZooKreepers Getting Fit, VEGGIE ZooKreepers*, and it goes on and on. So, I joined all of them! Or as many that I could. Now, this group that the photo was posted in could have been a 'secret' group. That means that it's invite only. Zookreeper is a slang term for the night shift zookeepers. So, I joined all these groups hoping to find the true original origin of the photo."

There are werewolf legends adjacent to Amarillo as well. Though the city sits well beyond the bounds of the Triangle, there are sightings listed on modern websites in Oklahoma and New Mexico. There are also folk tales, some like the older encounters detailed in this volume, of werewolf-like creatures outside the state of Texas but geographically near Amarillo. Oklahoma has a smattering of Dogman-like sightings, not to mention ample other examples of paranormal phenomena and folklore. Tangentially, one might pursue an infinite avenue of questioning in relation to this case.

Ashley made observations like my own regarding the city of Amarillo's handling of the photo:

"Amarillo did post about the photo on social media but were very careful not to claim it and have not spoken to any investigators about it. They likely enjoyed the publicity. I'm a bit far from Texas, but I would love to see a fellow Fortean go check the place out, visit the zoo, and just start asking the employees what the word on the street is."[36]

---

[36] At time of writing the Amarillo Dogman remains an unsolved case, with no corporate or singular entity claiming credit for it.

24

The Monsters of Medina

Now - let's get into Dogman.

Medina Lake in Bandera County is closely adjacent to San Antonio. Once a popular destination for all manner of aquatic recreation, the 18-mile-long reservoir has seen its water levels recede drastically in recent years. In February of 2023 local news station KENS5 reported that the lake's water level had dropped 33.5 feet versus a year prior, and this was hardly a new trend. This once verdant landscape is drying up.

Nick Losoya lives almost on the banks of Medina Lake, and he has been in the area for years.

"Of course, there's no water here now." he says with a sardonic chuckle. But the receding waters of the Medina are not the only strange activity to cross Nick's radar.

"I've been noticing changes around my neighborhood. We used to have tons of feral cats, and they've been disappearing."

He pauses before adding,

"Stuff's been going on here."

Nick is a fifth generation Texas native. He is of Apache descent and has spent much of his life hearing stories of dark creatures lurking in the isolated reaches of the Texas hill country.

I first met Nick in September of 2022 after we were introduced by Joe Doyle. As mentioned, this would be far from the only time Jessi and Joe of Hellbent Holler would assist me in this project. Nick has had an interest in

Sasquatch for several years, but recently the Dogman phenomena has come to the forefront of his attention. His brushes with unknown creatures however begin much earlier, nearly fifty years before he and I would meet.

"We had a property down south in Lytle, Texas. For some reason us kids were home by ourselves. I hear my sister screaming and hollering, and I hear the German Shepherd going crazy. So in my mind I'm thinking the German Shepherd turned on my sister, because of the way it sounded. So I ran and grabbed the rifle."

Nick burst out of the house, his sister making a frantic flight towards the front door as he emerged.

"She mentioned a 'giant bird' tried to pick her up."

Nick was incredulous.

"Back then we only had encyclopedias. So, I opened the book on the birds, 'point out the bird that tried to pick you up.' Well, she pointed out a pterodactyl. So, I said okay, and I left it alone."

Nick's sister would stand by the story into adulthood. Stories of "thunderbirds" have circulated in cryptozoology circles for years, and the state of Texas is no exception. There are even other tales of them attempting to abduct human children, but like many topics we have touched on, this is one for another volume.

"Now - let's get into Dogman."

Nick starts off by letting me know that his father had an encounter he described as looking like a massive timber wolf in the 60s. The beast moved on four legs but was of such massive proportions as to defy any other specimen the witness had seen.

Nick also reminds me, "There's no timber wolves in Texas."

Another story of an encounter was relayed to him by a friend in 2020.

"He went outside about 3 o'clock, two in the morning, and he saw something by the stream. And he saw the head, it was canine, so right away he ran in to get his pistol and a camera.

"He thought it was a bear, but there's no bears here. So, he thought man it's a hog, but it was too big."

Before the man could train either his camera or his firearm on the creature, it took off. But rather than fleeing into the stream or deeper into the woods, the animal instead pursued a vertical escape.

"It was running up the ravine, like a cliff. It was moving fast."

Nick's work as a business owner takes him across the Hill Country. He's often invited to locations where visitors are not generally welcome, and has developed a hobby out of asking his customers: "Have you ever seen anything strange out here?"

He's received a variety of responses, but shortly before our conversation one man had responded simply,

"You should talk to my daughter."

Nick did. A meeting was arranged.

"'Yeah, I saw something,'" she said, "'my husband makes fun of me - says it was my imagination.'"

The witness is a nurse at an area hospital and was on her way home from a late shift in 2020 at approximately 2:30 in the morning.

"She was driving, and as she was going across that bridge, she noticed something squatted down. It had roadkill in its palms, and it was eating. She described it and said it looked like a werewolf."[37]

Nick states that this encounter took place on the west side of Medina Lake off highway 173, and it would not be a singular occurrence.

"About a month after that a coworker of hers was coming home on the same road, about the same time. She saw it, and this time it was running across the road."

I asked Nick to clarify how, exactly, the creature was running.

"This was on two legs."

Two sightings in one location are interesting enough, but a third would be reported a short time later.

"Three to four miles from that location some people moved into that area."

Nick was called to the property to perform some work, and as he always does, chatted up the property owner with his usual inquiry.

"The only way you know is if you ask. And I asked them, you ever hear anything, ever see anything?"

The witness would go on to describe a third sighting, also involving the creature crossing the road on two legs, and off of Highway 173 west of Medina Lake. Nick speculates that the animals - if they are animals - use Bulverde Creek south of the Medina Lake Dam as a

---

[37] One may recall the first encounter detailed in this volume, taking place in Lampasas in 2018. A strikingly similar description and setting, and this one given by Mr. Losoya during our first conversation. Nick had seen none of my notes, and at time of writing had not read this manuscript.

passageway, availing themselves of the heavy vegetation to remain hidden and move about the region.

"They're traveling along the corridor in that area, south of the dam and the lake. They travel back and forth in that location. There's a lot of valleys. It's Hill Country - it's wooded, heavily wooded. There's deep ravines and valleys through there."

This mirrors the activity theorized by Rod Nichols very early in this book. His research would seem to indicate that a hypothetical Sasquatch or Dogman population might use heavily wooded areas near population centers as a safe means of passage. Medina Lake, however, is far less developed than San Antonio.

"If they head directly south of the dam, it heads towards Mico, Texas."

Despite this wealth of anecdotal evidence, Nick would relay one more tale that would give me frequent pause in the intervening days between our interview and the publication of the book you are now reading.

He tells a story of an unnamed victim killed by what he believes to be a Dogman, a government cover up, and an elusive video clip which has the potential to settle the Texas Dogman debate once and for all.

"My father-in-law is a retired marine, and he's good friends with the captain of the Division of Wildlife. One month before this incident happened to this young guy - who got killed - they had reports. There were sightings around the Brazos River."

The Brazos River runs from an area east of Stonewall County (northwest of Fort Worth) for 840 miles, finally meeting the ocean near Freeport, south of Houston.

Its route encompasses a cornucopia of cities, small towns, undeveloped areas, and everything in between. With nearly 900 miles of ground to cover, one can only wonder what may be lurking along the banks.

"They (officers of the Division of Wildlife) got on the river at night, had cameras around the boat, and put the boat on a trolling motor. Quietly.

"They heard something on the bank, and when he heard something, they fired up the spotlights. It was the Dogman. And they caught it on video. It was one month prior before that gentleman got killed."

Nick explains that an official statement regarding the victim's death was an attack by a large cat - perhaps a mountain lion - but as noted elsewhere, these creatures are not indigenous to the area in question. I was unable to find any reports online which correlate to the details of Nick's story, but if indeed a coverup is in play, perhaps we should not be surprised.

Naturally, I asked Nick if he had the video. After almost two years of diehard research, the possibility of a clear film of this primordial horror - even if only for a second or a few frames - set me to salivating as the creature itself might over a fresh carcass. With such a close familial connection to the witnesses, would he have managed to obtain a copy or even see it?

"No, I've been trying to get it," Nick says "but they're not gonna let that go. I'm ex-DOD myself. NORAD."

Nick accepts silence on the part of the powers that be as an inevitability, hardly worth being rattled over. This is often the case with ex-military members, as the handling of sensitive information is an integral part of any enlisted person or officer's training. Somewhere in my mind, a small voice sighed and said *of course.*

Were one to obtain this footage, many questions may be put to rest. Sadly, this has yet to prove possible. But with so many encounters taking place in the Medina Lake area, and with so many potential hiding spots along the Brazos, we may yet find that one critical piece of evidence. The lynchpin in the hunt for the Texas Dogman:

Proof.

25

Mundane Explanations

There are several answers to the Dogman question which would seem to negate its status as an otherworldly or inexplicable happening. In my talks I have heard many opinions regarding what a Dogman (or werewolf) is, and many, *many* more guesses as to what we might be seeing - assuming of course that the existence of an upright wolf is, as many people will sadly conclude, off the table.

Most readily at hand is the write-off of misidentification. The simple answer is that witnesses are seeing one thing, but due to exhaustion, fear, or intoxication are perceiving something else, most likely when confronted by a known species of animal.
Wolves and coyotes are the first to come to mind. Bears are also an option. A primate could be responsible for some of these sightings but given that primates are not native to the American Southwest, this answer is almost as strange as the question.[38] Moose are enormous animals and seen at night and in flight may appear to be canine. We may write at least this one off almost completely in the case of the Texas Dogman Triangle, as moose do not live in the state. It is far too hot - a moose can become overheated at 60 degrees Fahrenheit, while the average temperature in Texas during summer of 2022 was somewhere between 95-105 degrees.

There are many breeds of domestic dog which could fit the bill. German Shepherds, Belgian Malanois, Irish Wolfhound, Grand Pyranese, various Pit Bull breeds, some varieties of Rottweiler, Cane Corso, Mastiffs, Huskies, and wolf/dog hybrids (just to name a few) can reach truly monstrous proportions. With the proper diet and

---

[38] Bigfoot notwithstanding, of course.

preventative veterinary care any one of these breeds can easily grow to a size which, in the dark and under duress, could be perceived as "werewolf sized."

The problem with this is that wild dogs do not have access to preventative veterinary care, and their diets are dependent upon what they can catch. Almost all sightings of wolfman forms take place in isolated areas, further indicating the presence of a wild animal, not a domesticated one.

Perhaps it goes without saying, but these breeds also do not possess the ability to walk on two legs. While there may be exceptions, such as in cases of injury or illness as mentioned by Courteney in Chapter 4, the organisms confronting the witnesses in almost all these encounters display an ability to walk comfortably on two legs. In addition, some of the breeds mentioned are muscular and stocky, but would not appear to be six, eight, or even ten-feet-tall when rising on two legs.

Next is the idea of mental illness. Humanity is barely reaching a point where we can comfortably discuss this uncomfortable topic, but for the sake of our survival, it is necessary that we learn to do so. We cannot immediately dismiss the notion that some of these witnesses may be suffering from a psychological malady which causes them to perceive a monstrous upright form where there is none. This does not, however, explain why so many report the same things. It also does not present a sufficient challenge to encounters where the witness is known to the person receiving the report, as has been the case for both me and other researchers of these bizarre proceedings. It is simply not good enough to suppose that these people are mentally ill, and to assume such could very easily be called disrespectful.

The third in our gallery of explanations is intoxication. It is not a rare occurrence for the witness of unusual experiences, including Dogman encounters, to assure their interviewer that they were not under the influence of any psychoactive substances. One will hear this from every breed of paranormal experiencer imaginable, and their insistence is often noted in books and podcasts and TV shows and so on. Witnesses feel the need to assure us that they were not drunk or high, but I would present a touch of devil's advocacy on this excuse.

Just because a person has consumed some amount of a psychoactive substance does not mean they are not seeing something truly strange. Alcohol, unless consumed in extremely drastic quantities or in high concentrations, does not make people hallucinate. Neither does marijuana nor any number of other controlled substances. That is not to ignore the fact that there can always be exceptions to the effects such substances have on an individual as every person has different body chemistry. In addition, of course, there are drugs and combinations of drugs which can make a person hallucinate. However, gaining access to these substances is not as simple as strolling into a pharmacy. In most of these cases, when one examines the witnesses closely, it becomes a stretch to assume that they were using mushrooms or acid at the time that they experienced an oddity.

There is also a growing belief in the paranormal community that use of certain intoxicants may enhance a person's perception or sensitivity to the inexplicable. We will not try to make this case, but it should be kept in mind before any strange encounter is dismissed under assumption that the witness was intoxicated.

A somewhat more ethereal explanation is that these images may be hard-wired into our psyche and that some of us cannot help but see them. Psychologist Carl Jung wrote often of a concept he referred to as the *Collective Unconscious*. In his seminal work *The Red Book*, which is a collection of his writings from 1915 to 1930, Jung presents the fantastical hypothesis that all human beings share certain concepts, or "archetypes" buried in the back of our thinking brains. These archetypes shape how we view reality, tell our stories, and forge our own personalities. The various cards in Tarot may be considered something of a representation of these archetypes.

Perhaps so many human beings see werewolves because we carry them with us in our minds. Perhaps they have been with us since the dawn of known history because they are, quite literally, a part of us - just not in the sense that we can transform into them.[39]

Finally, we come to the explanation of a relic specimen of some prehistoric species. Dire wolves once lived in Texas, and their fossilized remains can still be found circa the rocky crags of Guadalupe Peak. Scientists estimate that they would have averaged in weight exceeding 100 pounds, near 200 in some cases. It seems, however, that they were also rather short on all fours. They stood within the range of just a little over two feet at the shoulder.

Another long extinct hound - and one which we should be grateful that we do not have to contend with in the modern-day - is the Amphicyon. This daikaiju of a brute was a member of an extinct family of mammals known as Amphicyonidae, or more simply described as "Bear Dogs." The Amphicyon was the largest known subspecies. They are believed to have grown to an average of eight feet in length, and to weigh as much as 1,400 pounds. A one thousand- and four-hundred-pound Bear Dog…a horrifying concept!

Problematically, Amphicyon fossils have only been found in Europe, but these are only two examples. Bear Dogs are believed to have roamed the earth for millions

---

[39] This is a gross simplification of the Collective Unconscious. Readers are encouraged to dive into the topic at their leisure. This volume lacks the space, and its writer lacks the intellect to properly examine it.

upon millions of years before humanity came along to spoil the party. One can speculate a great deal about what other monstrous ursine hounds may have tyrannized the prehistoric world.

Most aficionados of Dogman phenomena would be overjoyed if the dire wolf, Amphicyon, or any of their innumerable cousins turned out to be the source of these reports. The existence of a living member of a species believed extinct would not only bring greater credibility to cryptozoology as a science (rather than, as some dismiss it, a pseudoscience), but also it would mark a discovery just as strange and wondrous as the werewolf itself.

Regardless, none of these explanations have sufficiently answered the werewolf question. Reports continue to stack on and add more weight to the phenomena. However, to some of those harboring doubt, the old write-offs seem less potent and less believable than the purportedly fantastic.

26

The Hybrid Theory

In the book *Beast - Werewolves, Serial Killers, and Man-Eaters: The Mystery of the Monsters of the Gevaudan*, which is a deep and fascinating dive into the story of the Beast of Gevaudan, the authors posit an interesting theory. This theory may have relevance to the strange goings on in the Texas wilderness.

For those not familiar with *La Bête du Gévaudan*, a quick explanation is necessary. This story is often mixed in with werewolf lore and mentioned alongside other encounters with strange canines. The fact that 300 years have gone, and the world is still debating the nature of the thing should indicate just how distinctive this story is.

In the 1700s, a French province known as the Gevaudan was terrorized by a four-legged demon of a wolf beast. The monster attacked and killed over 100 people, many of them young children. The fiend would forgo easy prey such as lambs or goats and go out of its way to attack the human beings which watched over them. It was a grisly affair. Reports described the beast as a large, wolf-like creature and theories ranged across the spectrum as to what it might be. A hyena was one possible explanation. An armored wolf another - the animal was apparently resistant to gunfire, much like our Texan Dogmen - and even more exotic speculation such as a true, transforming werewolf. In the end, two animals were eventually killed and paraded into the court of King Louis. Whether either was the dreaded *La Bête* will never be known.

One chapter in this book concerns various theories regarding *La Bête's* nature. One is of a hybrid wolf/canine. The authors note that there have been numerous cases of "outlaw wolves" in the history of North America, and that the great majority of them, when captured or killed, bore both wolf and dog-like traits.

They cite the work of zoologists who posit that a canine hybrid may be larger than either of its parent species, regardless of the breed of domestic dog in question, and reference numerous examples. Such interbreeding could also account for aberrant behavior, and in the case of The Beast, the unnatural attacks on human beings.

Is it possible that the upright wolves seen in Texas are some sort of hybrid species? An intermixture of the various subspecies that make up the predators of Texas? Previously examined are the Galveston Wolves, a known hybrid. We have also discussed the Texas Terror Dog, another frightful beast with a well-documented history. The Terror Dog especially has been purported to feast on blood - might this aberrant behavior be due to a misalignment of its genetics, due to repeated interbreeding between various canine species?

La Bête du Gévaudan preferred human beings, even though they pose a greater threat than your average lamb. Young children may be an exception, but even the youngsters of Gevaudan would carry pikes and other simple weapons as defense against wild animals. In one particularly harrowing account of the Beast's reign of terror, it was fought off by a group of children thusly armed. One of the few stories wherein its victims survived the assault.

In Lockhart, we met the Beast of Plum Creek, who was said to have made a habit of "disemboweling" the local livestock. Presumably it also fed upon them. The gory scenes described by the ranchers of Plum Creek would seem to go beyond normal predatory behavior in an almost sadistic fashion.

We have learned that some of the more exotic canine hybrids might not be capable of long term, generational reproduction. As Courteney mentioned and Sara would later corroborate, some mixes are infertile due to their genetics. If the source of these werewolf sightings is in fact some unknown canine mixture, infertility could account for our not having formally classified them.

Suppose that occasionally the right animals cross bloodlines under the right circumstances, and one or more of their offspring develops an affinity for bipedal locomotion. Suppose these beasts do not live long, or that they make it a point to stay away from human populations. Suppose also that when they eventually die, they decompose and/or their remains are incorrectly labeled as belonging to a normal canine species. This cannot be proven, but it may be plausible.

This is only one hypothesis. The world is far stranger than we will likely ever know, but the hybrid theory does at least have some foundation in known zoological science.

27

Common Denominators

There are many recurring themes when one reviews summaries of purported Dogman activity. Much like UFO sightings, run-ins with Sasquatch, suspected hauntings, visits from the Men in Black and many other inexplicable events, researching multiple accounts from multiple witnesses yields a pattern of physicality, behavior, and, in most cases, response from the human experiencers. Even if half of these encounters have been falsified (which the author severely doubts), there are still multiple examples of overlapping facets, repeated in story after story, throughout the Texas Dogman saga and especially within the Triangle. The purpose of this chapter will be to break down and analyze as many of these common denominators as possible. They are also divided by category, in what may be a vain attempt to present some semblance of organization. These criteria were applied in the process of including and eliminating potential Dogman encounters from the map of the Triangle and are presented as such.

Perhaps the reader will find these criteria, presented in a checklist format, helpful in examining their own Dogman/werewolf/wolfman/cynocephalus encounters, or any they may happen to hear of. It may also be helpful in separating reports of Sasquatch from reports of wolfmen.

Evidence

There are a few things which enhance the veracity of any story. These could also be categorized as different types of evidence, but in my research, I have been vigilant in watching for specific qualifiers in numerating these encounters. A few things that can make for a convincing sighting (not just in Dogman phenomena but across the cryptozoological spectrum) are:

- Eyewitness testimony
- Independent witness testimony (people who do not know each other or did not know each other before the event)
- Photographic evidence (still pictures or video)
- Footprints, claw marks, or signs of vandalism
- Credible witnesses (and their names)
- Documentation by media
- Response from law enforcement
- Repeated occurrences
- Verifiable details (weather on the date in question, specific location details such as intersecting roads, nearby towns, parks, and water sources)

Not all of these are required for a story to be compelling, but the more of them are present, the better off we are. Some of the more infamous cryptid or unsolved cases of the last century, such as the Mothman, the Hopkinsville Goblins, The Caracas Dwarves, and the Flatwoods Monster (as well as the accompanying Frametown Incident which took place near to Flatwoods) can check off at least three of these boxes. Sadly, I have yet to encounter a report of Dogmen in Texas that meets every single one, though a few have come close (San Benito and Dallas/Fort Worth, for example).

Physiology

The entities' physical traits are the most immediately evident, and in instances of visual sightings, seem to be what most witnesses remark upon first. In report after report witnesses describe upright ears. They notice sharp teeth, and often remark upon the claws. Yellow eyes are also a common cosmetic feature, though we have examples of "death black" eyes and even some which are bright blue, red, or green. The monsters seem to be equally comfortable locomoting on two legs as they are on four and can switch between these postures at apparent will. A muscular build is frequently mentioned, as are exaggerated forelimbs, a watchful gaze and thick fur. When the tail is brought up, words such as bobbed, short, and bushy come into play, but tails are not often mentioned. Are Dogman tails generally so short that they aren't noticeable? Are there sub-breeds of Dogmen with varying tail lengths as there are with ordinary domestic dogs?

Physical features commonly noted and described by witnesses include:

- Exceeding a height of five feet (while on two legs)
- Exceptionally long bodies (when on four legs)
- Sharp or pointed ears
- Thick or shaggy fur
- An intense stare, often making eye contact
- A noticeably muscular build
- Sharp or prominent teeth
- Bipedal locomotion

- Apparent resistance to gunfire, even at close range
- Yellow or amber eyes

Behavior

The exotic life forms we have examined also undeniably exhibit recurring patterns of behavior. The actions of these beings are not always in sync with other sightings, but there are quite a few aspects which are repeated on numerous occasions. Such as:

- Aggression towards other animals, particularly domestic dogs
- Aggression towards humans, whether in the form of violence, pursuit, or vocalization
- Unnaturally loud, distinct howling or barking
- "Stare downs" with human experiencers (once again, eye contact, an intimidation act in most canines)
- Crouching beside or crossing roads, usually at night
- Persistence: they frequently return to the location of previous sightings, even after being shot
- Predation of livestock
- Lack of fear of humans, firearms, electric lights, and automobiles

Sounds

In cases where they are said to vocalize, we see a recurrence of huffing sounds, growling, and guttural not-quite-human-not-quite-canine screaming. The sounds are generally portrayed as being unsettling or frightening and often deep in tone. Also, on the topic of noise, the ambient sounds of the outdoors are often noted by witnesses as falling strangely, eerily silent.

- Unnaturally loud canine howls
- "Screams," sometimes described as human like
- Huffing or heavy breathing
- Heavy footfalls or stomping sounds when the creatures are moving, loud enough to be heard from indoors
- Eerie silence in the area where the sighting occurs; other nature sounds often disappear, despite the thick vegetation of most of these locations.
- Sounds of distress from other canines (contrasting with the strange silence noted above)

Proximity to Food Sources

Most of these sightings occur in areas with thick greenbelts, providing an apex predator with an abundance of things to hunt. If these beings are, in fact, organic in nature and not from another planet or another dimension, then they certainly require food to survive. There is also a heavy presence of whitetail deer in areas where modern sightings are closely bunched, such as the outer rim of Dallas/Fort Worth, the Wolf Mountain Cluster near Austin and Sam Houston National Forest. In truth, these skittish herbivores inhabit most of the state. Witness descriptions of long claws, pointed teeth, forward facing eyes and up-pointed ears would seem to verify a predatory diet, as these anatomical features are evolved to accommodate. A few examples of Texas fauna which may provide a viable food source include:

- Whitetail Deer
- Wild Hogs
- Rabbits
- Mice
- Rats
- Domestic pets
- Livestock (mammalian and fowl)
- Various species of fish (Bears can snatch fish from a stream - why not a werewolf?)
- Various species of bird
- People (?)

Locations

Speaking of the places where sightings occur, one thing which is almost always the same in these stories is the topography. Numerous parallels can be drawn in the locations of nearly all instances where a human crosses paths with a lycanthrope. Streams and lakes come up again and again, as do caves and limestone bluffs, which provide sources of fresh water and concealment respectively. In general, an animal whose makeup is based in the canine realm will be right at home in the woods and on the plains.

- Heavily wooded areas
- Commonly in proximity to national parks

- Generally near a water source (often seen while fishing or camping near a lake)
- Heavy presence of caves and ridges; limestone covers much of the Texan landscape
- Rural, undeveloped spaces
- Often near farms or homesteads
- In proximity to the locations of folktales involving upright wolves or strange bipeds

Witness Response

It probably goes without saying that in addition to all of these, Dogmen are never described as "friendly," leaving impressions of malice and danger with the human beings who spot them. The reactions of witnesses are some of the most telling pieces of evidence, and we will explore this further in the next chapter. In general, however, experiencers of this frightening spectacle repeat several key behaviors. Both conscious and subconscious responses can be observed such as:

- The feeling of being watched
- Opening fire on the creature if the witness has a weapon on hand
- Seeking out a weapon if one is not on hand
- Running away
- Feelings of paralysis
- Intense feelings of fear, dread, or panic

Most, if not all of this makes sense if we are dealing with an unclassified species. It may or may not make sense if we are dealing with a spiritual or preternatural entity, but we currently lack sufficient verifiable information for either conclusion. Regardless, every land-dwelling mammal that we are aware of requires food, water, protection from the elements, and sufficient space to live away from large scale urban centers and heavy human populations. All the locations examined in this volume, with some exception, contain all these necessities in abundance.

An overlap of any or all these various criteria make for a compelling, terrifying story. Some things, such as photographic evidence, are hard to locate and do not appear often. Others, such as howling noises and bipedal locomotion, are repeated almost *ad infinitum*.

It is the final element noted above which must now become the focus of our study, as its importance cannot, or at least should not, be downplayed. To do so may prove deadly, as it did for the farmer's son in Converse:

The element of **fear**.

28

The Element of Fear

Almost every sighting of suspected Dogmen or werewolves or wolfmen is punctuated by the witness describing an overpowering sense of fear. Like in stories of meetings with the aforementioned Black-Eyed Kids, witnesses almost always leave the encounter shaken to their very core. Some report lingering effects after the fact, such as fear of the woods, discomfort in the dark, and general skittishness. This is in addition to symptoms that could very easily be equated to Post Traumatic Stress Disorder. Jeremiah Byron, creator and host of the Bigfoot Society podcast, sums it up well,

"My opinion on the Dogman phenomena is that people are seeing something in the woods that is affecting them in ways that other cryptids aren't."

Jeremiah has conducted hundreds of interviews during his short and still burgeoning career. He started the Bigfoot Society podcast a little over three years ago (as of 2023), and his gallery of previous guests includes Cliff Barackman, Shannon Legro, Seth Breedlove, and many of the specialists interviewed for this book. It may be that no one has asked more questions about cryptozoology as of the year 2023 than Mr. Byron.

"There is definitely a creature out there that seems to be entirely negative in its outlook on life, and it's taking that out on people that it meets."

Witnesses and other researchers would seem to agree. In prior chapters we spoke with Jessi and Joe Doyle of Hellbent Holler. One may recall that they have had, and even captured on thermal imaging, their own sightings of

inexplicable canine forms while investigating the fabled
Land Between the Lakes and had this to say:

"I would have much rather that we had encountered
something along the lines of a traditional Sasquatch. It
would have been easier to swallow."

The fight or flight instinct that we all share must
play a role in this. Human beings are naturally inclined to
identify potential threats, so it makes sense that witnesses
would frequently remark on claws, teeth, a predatory stare,
and savage howls. In most cases the witness chooses flight,
but we do see examples (John near Dallas/Fort Worth,
Bobby in Vidor, the anonymous witness in Freestone
County, and Jeff in Collin County) where fight becomes the
chosen course. In three of these cases, the animals seem to
shrug off direct gunfire. John dispensed multiple rounds
into the animal he described as a juvenile male, and Bobby
shot one at point blank range with a .12-gauge shotgun. The
unnamed witness in Freestone County took at least one shot
at the unidentified animal they saw with the aid of a scope.
Jeff did not open fire upon the creature, but reports that his
neighbor did, only to have it return a short time later. In
cases where witnesses do not run away from these animals,
they deem it necessary to engage them in combat. One can
hardly blame John and Bobby for employing the use of
firearms in their responses - after all, their homes and
persons had come under direct assault. Bobby had already
lost more than one dog, and John is the sentinel of a large
quantity of livestock.

Is there some ingrained evolutionary necessity that
makes us afraid of these seemingly impossible beasts?
Almost certainly, in the same way we would be afraid
when coming face to face with a lion, tiger, wild boar or
rabid dog. It may also be connected to the werewolf's

recurrence in the literature and folklore of so many cultures throughout human history. Is there something buried within our collective psyche that forces us to acknowledge the threat posed by the werewolf, even if it is imagined? We should again consider the concept of a *Collective Unconscious*. Is this fear response inevitable, whether we consume the werewolf as a Hollywood invention or experience a confrontation with it ourselves? Do we remember, perhaps better than we realize, what our ancestors learned through dire misfortune?

Perhaps the "paranormal" aspect of these run-ins should be given further consideration. Experiencers of ghost and poltergeist activity, UAP phenomena, abduction encounters, and of course, run-ins with Bigfoot report similar feelings of terror and discomfort. What makes Dogman encounters unique is that this impression of horror seems to arise in almost every case (except for Killian's sighting near Conroe), while there are plenty of stories paired with other phenomena described as positive by the experiencers.[40]

Discounting the importance of the fear experienced by the witnesses in almost every Dogman or similar encounter may be a dangerous step. It seems very likely that whether these entities are physical animals, interdimensional interlopers, or non-corporeal spirits, humans are strongly inclined towards running away from them. We have discussed two encounters in this book where a Dogman-like creature charged at a human being (John and Bobby, as mentioned), and two more in which someone was allegedly killed (the farmer's son in Converse and the unnamed man in Bandera County).

---

[40] An exception here, perhaps, is abduction phenomena, but that is yet another study for another time.

I hesitate to ask the next question for fear of one day finding out:

How many people have been unlucky enough to meet one of these savage canids whose stories we will never hear, because there is no one alive to tell them?

As stated early in this volume, we no longer live alongside the wolves. We no longer fear them, at least not as an aspect of our daily lives. Perhaps, at least for people living in certain areas, near thick stretches of vegetation and large bodies of water, near-infinite acreages, sprawling national parks and the many isolated warrens of the Texas Hill Country, this mentality should be reassessed. While certainly no one should live in fear, perhaps some of us should live with a bit more caution.

Especially those of us living within the Texas Dogman Triangle.

Epilogue

This work represents the foundation lain by all parties interviewed, quoted, and credited herein. My role has been to collect these stories and present them in a somewhat organized fashion, compare them to one another, and do so in a way which I hope has been entertaining. But it is the original chroniclers of these encounters, and of course the witnesses who experienced them, who have made the actual discoveries. As such, I have made a concerted effort to credit each source appropriately. It is important to note that the opinions expressed in this book are my own, unless otherwise stated, and permission was given by all parties interviewed to be mentioned, quoted, or otherwise included in this volume. My gratitude to each and every one of them is difficult to adequately express but suffice to say this book would not exist without their assistance.

While I had hoped to compile as comprehensive a volume as possible, there are other accounts, stories, and reports of unpleasant wolfish specters in the state of Texas. One website showcases an interactive Google map not unlike that of the North American Dogman Project, but I was unable to contact the administrator and obtain permission to include its data. Some of these could be sourced elsewhere and are included, such as the Converse and Vidor cases, but a small sampling of these secondhand accounts has been omitted from this text. There are also other sightings detailed on blogs and podcasts of additional frightening manwolf activity in Texas, and while attempts were made to contact these witnesses and include their testimony, life does not always organize itself to our convenience.

I am, however, glad to say with relative confidence that the majority of the data available on Dogman encounters in Texas is at least mentioned here, to the extent that I have been able to ascertain. While I have certainly missed something somewhere and hope to continue to learn more - it was not possible to listen to every episode of every paranormal podcast, read every book on cryptozoology, watch every YouTube video, or read every blog post on the internet - it is this collection of folk tales, photographs, newspaper clippings and eyewitness accounts which have cemented in my mind a statement made very early in this book:

Werewolves are real, and they live in Texas.

Resources

Timeline of Encounters

Map of Dogman Encounters in Texas

Recommended Reading

Bibliography and Cited Sources

Timeline of Encounters

(* denotes encounters that fall outside the area which this book defines as the Texas Dogman Triangle)

The Beast of Bear Creek – 1800s

The Converse Wolfman – 1800s

Orange - 1933

Greggton* – 1958

Meridian State Park – 1977

Sam Houston National Forest - 1977

Plum Creek – 1980

Kerrville – 1980

Sanger – 1985

Bluetown* – 1990s

Paradise - 1996

McAllen* - 2008

San Benito* - 2013

Fredericksburg – 2016

Freestone County - 2016

Lampasas – 2018

Collin County - 2018

Sam Houston National Forest – Various dates, 2018

Medina Lake* - Various dates, 2020

The Brazos River - 2020

Fredericksburg - 2020

Pedernales Falls State Park – 2020

Dallas/Fort Worth - 2021-2022

Conroe - 2022

Amarillo* - 2022

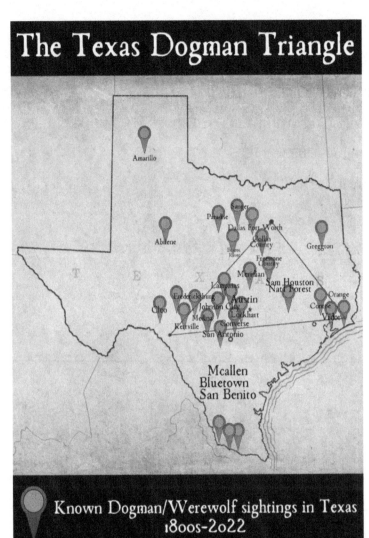

Recommended Reading

The author recommends the following resources to those interested in the Dogman phenomenon. These resources are also valuable for inquiries of many alternative natures but proved indispensable during the research phase of The Texas Dogman Triangle, or in some cases, have proven instrumental in framing my personal perspective towards the unsolved. This is not an exhaustive list, but it is a wonderful start for the curious cryptozoologist.

Websites

North American Dogman Project

True Horror Stories of Texas

Texas Cryptid Hunter

Texashillcountry.com

The Texas History Portal

The Cloaked Hedgehog

Books

I Know What I Saw by Linda S Godfrey

The Beast of Bray Road by Linda S Godfrey

Real Wolfmen of America by Linda S Godfrey (as well as just about anything else by Linda S Godfrey)

Shapeshifters by Nick Redfern

Chupacabra Road Trip by Nick Redfern

Monsters of Texas by Ken Gerhard and Nick Redfern

Features and Fillers: Texas Journalists on Texas Folklore from The Texas Folklore Society (by various contributing authors)

The Encyclopedia of Vampires, Werewolves, And Other Monsters by Rosemary Ellen Guiley

The Vengeful Djinn by Rosemary Ellen Guiley and Philip Imbrogno

Werewolves: Encounters with the Black Dog by Joedy Cook

Beast: Werewolves, Serial Killers, and Man-Eaters: The Mystery of the Monsters of the Gévaudan by S. R. Schwalb and Gustavo Sánchez Romero

Hunt for the Skinwalker by George Knapp and Colm A Kelleher

The Eighth Tower by John Keel

Strange Creatures from Time and Space by John Keel

Dictionary of Mythology by Bergen Evans

Classical Mythology by Mark PO Morford and Robert J Lenardon

Metroplex Monsters by Jason McClean

Podcasts

Bigfoot Society Podcast

The Cryptochats Podcast

On Wednesdays, We Talk Weird

Hellbent Holler

Hey Strangeness

Unrefined

Fright Life Paranormal

Films/documentaries

Skinwalker: Howl of the Rougarou

American Werewolves

The Bray Road Beast

The Werewolf Experiments

The Man Wolf Files

Sources

Introduction

https://www.texasmonthly.com/travel/red-wolves-texas-breeding-program/

https://truehorrorstoriesoftexas.com/

https://northamericandogmanproject.com/

Chapter 1

https://www.kxan.com/news/unsolved-the-mysteries-lurking-in-lake-travis/

https://www.kut.org/energy-environment/2011-06-17/dead-alligator-found-on-shores-of-lake-travis

https://www.cbssports.com/nfl/news/browns-baker-mayfield-claims-he-almost-100-percent-saw-a-ufo/

https://www.austintexas.org/film-commission/permits-and-regulations/drone-regulations/

BOOK: *Black Eyed Kids* by David Weatherly

BOOK: *True Tales of The Unknown* by Sharon Jarvis

Chapter 2

BOOK: *Chupacabra Road Trip* by Nick Redfern

BOOK: *Monsters of Texas* by Nick Redfern and Ken Gerhard

https://www.mysanantonio.com/entertainment/article/san-antonio-chupacabra-elemendorf-beast-16350028.php

https://mexicanfolklorewitnessaccounts.wordpress.com/2018/04/24/the-hounds-of-hell-el-paso-tx-pheonix-az-warning-not-for-the-faint-hearted/

https://ghostcitytours.com/galveston/ghost-stories/jean-lafitte/

https://www.chron.com/news/houston-texas/article/Galveston-ghost-wolves-red-wolves-17367033.php#:~:text=At%20least%20four%20distinct%20groups,DNA%20while%20others%20have%20less

https://www.nps.gov/jela/learn/nature/upload/Mammals%20of%20Barataria.pdf

Chapter 3

BOOK: Tom Slick: True Life Encounters in Cryptozoology by Loren Coleman (revised edition)

BOOK: Monsters of Texas by Nick Redfern and Ken Gerhard

https://m.imdb.com/title/tt0824056/fullcredits/cast?ref_=tt_ov_st_sm (SWRI ep/Modern Marvels)

https://visitjeffersontexas.com/bigfoot-in-jefferson

https://snprc.org/

Chapter 4

Hellbent Holler (Youtube)

Hey Strangeness (Podcast)

Chapter 5

Interview with "Trent"

https://northamericandogmanproject.com/

https://www.alltrails.com/trail/us/texas/wolf-mountain-trail

https://visitmarblefalls.org/discover/wolf-mountain-trail

Chapter 6

https://texashistory.unt.edu/ark:/67531/metadc38313/m1/177/?q=%22rance%20moore%22

http://www.texasescapes.com/TexasHillCountryTowns/Cleo-Texas.htm

Chapter 7

https://truehorrorstoriesoftexas.com/

https://dailytimes.com/history/article_7a6d5b2c-f8fc-11e9-a0ba-8fb0db802a73.html

https://www.heb.com/static-page/article-template/Our-Story

Chapter 8

Interview with John

https://truehorrorstoriesoftexas.com/

Chapter 9

BOOK: *Real Wolfmen: True Encounters in Modern American* by Linda S Godfrey

Hellbent Holler (Youtube)

https://bridgehunter.com/tx/denton/180610AA0152002/

https://www.atlasobscura.com/places/goatmans-bridge

https://texashillcountry.com/donkey-lady-bridge-san-antonio/

https://u.osu.edu/popelickmonster/

Chapter 10

BOOK: *Monsters of Texas* by Nick Redfern and Ken Gerhard

http://texascryptidhunter.blogspot.com/2012/09/the-beast-of-bear-creek.html

https://texashistory.unt.edu/ark:/67531/metadc38313/m1/177/?q=%22rance%20moore%22

BOOK: *Quest for The Hexham Heads* by Paul Screeton

Chapter 11

http://texascryptidhunter.blogspot.com/2013/05/sasquatch-classics-converse-werewolf.html

BOOK: *Monsters of Texas* by Nick Redfern and Ken Gerhard

https://www.ksat.com/sa-live/2017/10/24/south-texas-haunted-folklore-the-tale-of-the-converse-werewolf/

Monstero Bizzarro Podcast: Southern Werewolves (Lyle Blackburn)

Chapter 12

The Austin American Statesman: May 29th, 1980

DOCUMENTARY: *The Dogman Triangle: Werewolves in the Lone Star State*

Chapter 13

https://northamericandogmanproject.com/

Chapter 14

https://northamericandogmanproject.com/

Chapter 15

https://northamericandogmanproject.com/

Chapter 16

https://www.fs.usda.gov/detail/texas/about-forest/districts/?cid=fswdev3_008443

https://tpwd.texas.gov/huntwild/hunt/wma/find_a_wma/list/?id=30

https://truehorrorstoriesoftexas.com/werewolf-like-creature-spotted-near-sam-houston-national-park/

https://www.reddit.com/r/dogman/comments/o3xp7q/just_c ome_back_from_a_camping_trip_in_the_wood_i/

DOCUMENTARY: *The Dogman Triangle: Werewolves in the Lone Star State*

Chapter 17

http://www.lyleblackburn.com/podcast.htm

https://northamericandogmanproject.com/documents

BOOK: *Monsters of Texas* by Nick Redfern and Ken Gerhard

Chapter 18

BOOK: *Monsters of Texas* by Nick Redfern and Ken Gerhard

Chapter 19

Interview with Killian Geiser

Chapter 20

WEBSITE: *True Horror Stories of Texas*

Interview with John Gonzales

Chapter 21

WEBSITE: *True Horror Stories of Texas*

Fate Magazine - March 1960

https://cmrosens.com/2020/03/30/werewolf-films-1950-1959/

https://www.imdb.com/list/ls032621399/

Chapter 22

North American Dogman Project

Chapter 23

https://www.amarillo.gov/Home/Components/News/News/2273/16

Interview with Ashley Hilt

Interview with Michael Mayes

https://www.statesman.com/story/news/local/2017/06/16/video-is-that-bigfoot-in/6667374007/

https://www.kxan.com/news/bigfoot-crossing-signs-go-up-in-round-rock/

https://www.statesman.com/story/news/local/2017/06/20/these-kids-went-looking-for/6667400007/

https://www.roundrocktexas.gov/news/parks-department-host-expedition-find-bigfoot-event/

https://patch.com/texas/round-rock/round-rock-officials-reveal-truth-sort-local-bigfoot-sightings

Chapter 24

https://www.edwardsaquifer.net/medina.html#:~:text=Medina%20Lake%20was%20constructed%20between,Antonio%2C%20just%20outside%20Loop%201604.

https://www.ksat.com/news/local/2023/02/16/aerial-footage-shows-a-nearly-dry-medina-lake-as-water-level-drops-below-6-capacity/#:~:text=SAN%20ANTONIO%20%E2%80%93%20Abandoned%20pontoon%20boats,to%20a%20multi%2Dyear%20drought.

https://www.tshaonline.org/handbook/entries/brazos-river#:~:text=The%20Brazos%20River%20rises%20at,95%C2%B023'%20W).

Interview with Nick Losoya

DOCUMENTARY: *The Dogman Triangle: Werewolves in the Lone Star State*

Chapter 25

https://www.nrdc.org/experts/andrew-wetzler/moose-dont-live-texas-or-how-global-warming-will-change-midwest#:~:text=Blog%20%E2%80%BA%20Andrew%20Wetzler-,Moose%20Don't%20Live%20in%20Texas%20(Or%20How%20Global,Warming%20Will%20Change%20the%20Midwest)&text=Illinois%20and%20Michigan.

https://www.gosanangelo.com/story/news/columnists/terry-maxwell/2017/01/08/naturally-texas-wolves-no-match-ranchers/96089586/

https://www.hmdb.org/m.asp?m=4759

https://www.livescience.com/56795-bear-dog.html

http://www.prehistoric-wildlife.com/species/a/amphicyon.html

Chapter 26

BOOK: *Beast - Werewolves, Serial Killers, and Man-Eaters: The Mystery of the Monsters of the Gevaudan* by Gustavo Sanchez Romero and S.R. Schwalb

Interview with Courteney Swihart

Interview with Sara Deese

Made in the USA
Monee, IL
22 January 2024

51591193R00136